MACBETH
Translated

SJ Hills

and

William Shakespeare

Faithfully Translated
into Performable Modern English

THE TRAGEDY OF MACBETH

Book 33 in a series of 42

This Work First Published In 2018
by DTC Publishing, London.
www.InteractiveShakespeare.com

Typeset by DTC Publishing.

Translated from Macbeth by Shakespeare, circa1606.

Revised 2021. A-XXVI

ISBN 978-1-731-27841-8

Interactive Shakespeare
Making the past accessible

SJ Hills Writing Credits: Dramatic Works.

Shakespeare Translated Series. Modern English With Original Text.
Faithfully translated line by line for students, actors and fans of Shakespeare.
Macbeth Translated
Romeo & Juliet Translated
Hamlet Translated
A Midsummer Night's Dream Translated
Othello Translated

Shakespeare For All Ages Series.
Modern English alongside simplified text and pictures. Suitable for the whole family. Faithfully translated line by line for students, adults and fans of all ages.
Macbeth For All Ages

Dramatised Classic Works.
Twenty-two dramatised works written and produced by SJ Hills for Encyclopaedia Britannica, based on classic stories including Shakespeare, for audiences of all ages around the world.
Greatest Tales of the World. Vol 1.
Greatest Tales of the World. Vol 2.

New Works Inspired By Classic Restoration Comedy Plays.
Scarborough Fair - inspired by *The Relapse*
To Take A Wife - inspired by *The Country Wife*
Wishing Well - inspired by *Epsom Wells*
Love In A Nunnery - inspired by *The Assignation.*

Modernised English Classic Works.
The Faerie Queene
Beowulf
The Virtuous Wife
Love's Last Shift
Wild Oats
The Way of the World

Dedicated to my four little terrors;
Melody
Eve
James
Hamilton

"From an ardent love of literature, a profound admiration of the men who have left us legacies of thought and beauty, and, I suppose, from that feature in man that induces us to strive to follow those we most admire, and looking upon the pursuit of literature as one of the noblest in which no labour should be deemed too great, I have sought to add a few thoughts to the store already bequeathed to the world. If they are approved, I shall have gained my desire; if not, I shall hope to receive any hints in the spirit of one who loves his work and desires to progress."

R. Hilton. 1869

PREFACE

When we studied Shakespeare at school we had to flick back and forth to the notes at the back of the book to understand a confusing line, words we were not familiar with, expressions lost in time, or even current or political references of Shakespeare's time.

What if the text was rewritten to make each line clear without looking up anything?

There are plenty of modern translations just for this. But they are cumbersome to read, no flow, matter of fact translations (and most are of varying inaccuracy, despite being approved by exam boards).

As a writer and producer of drama, I wanted not only to translate the play faithfully line by line, but also to include the innuendos, the political satire, the puns and the bawdy humour in a way which would flow and bring the work to life for students, actors prepping for a performance or lovers of the work to enjoy today, faithful to the feel and meaning of the original script and language.

A faithful line-by-line translation into modern phrasing that flows, along with additional staging directions and contextual notes, making the play interesting to read, easy to understand, and very importantly, an invaluable study aid.

For me it all started at about eight or nine years of age. I was reading a comic which contained the story of Macbeth serialised in simple comic strip form. I loved the story so much I could not wait to see what happened next so I rushed out to the public library to get a copy of the book. Of course, when I got it home I didn't even recognise it as being the same story. It made no sense to me, being written in 'Olde' English and often using 'flowery' language. I remember thinking at the time that one day I should write my version of the story for others to understand.

Years went by and I had pretty much forgotten my idea. Then quite by chance I was approached by Encyclopaedia Britannica to produce a series of dramatised classic dramas as educational aids for children learning English as a second language. Included in the selection was Romeo And Juliet which I was to condense down to fifty minutes using modern English.

This brought flooding back the memories of being eight years old again, reading my comic and planning my translated version of Shakespeare. In turn it also led me to the realisation that even if a reader could understand English well, this did not mean they could fully understand and enjoy Shakespeare. I could understand English, yet I did not fully understand some of Shakespeare's text without serious research, so what hope did a person whose first language was not English have?

After some investigation, I discovered there was a great desire around the world to understand the text fully without the inconvenience of referring to footnotes or sidelines, or worse still, the internet. How can one enjoy the wonderful drama with constant interruption? I was also surprised to discover the desire was equally as great in English speaking countries as ones whose first language was not English.

The final kick to get me started was meeting fans of Shakespeare's works who knew scripts off by heart but secretly admitted to me that they did have trouble fully understanding the meaning of some lines. Although they knew the storyline well they could miss some of the subtlety and innuendo Shakespeare was renowned for. It is hardly surprising in this day and age as many of the influences, trends, rumours, beliefs and current affairs of Shakespeare's time are not valid today.

I do not pretend my work is any match for the great master, but I do believe in the greater enjoyment for all. These great works deserve to be understood by all, Shakespeare himself wrote for all levels of audience, he would even aim his work to suit a particular audience at times – for example changing historical facts if he knew a member of royalty would be seeing his play and it would cause them any embarrassment, or of course to curry favour with a monarch by the use of flattery.

I have been as faithful as possible with my version, but the original, iambic pentameter, (the tempo and pace the lines were written for), and other Elizabethan tricks of the trade that Shakespeare was so brilliant at are not included unless vital to the text and meaning. For example, rhyming couplets to signify the end of a scene, for in Shakespeare's day there were no curtains, no lights and mostly static scenery, so scene changes were not so obvious. These couplets, though not strictly necessary, are included to maintain the feel of the original.

This makes for a play that sounds fresh to today's listening audience. It is also a valuable educational tool; English Literature courses often include a section on translating Shakespeare. I am often asked the meaning of a particular line, sometimes scholars argue over the meaning of particular lines. I have taken the most widely agreed version and the one which flows best with the story line where there is dispute, and if you read this translation before reading the original work or going to see a stage version, you will find the play takes on a whole new meaning, making it infinitely more enjoyable.

SJ Hills. London. 2018

Author's Note: This version contains stage directions. These are included purely as a guide to help understand the script better. Any director staging the play would have their own interpretation of the play and decide their own directions. These directions are my own personal interpretation and not those of Shakespeare. You may change these directions to your own choosing or ignore them completely. For exam purposes these should be only regarded as guidance to the dialogue and for accuracy should not be quoted in any studies or examinations.

I have also replaced the word *'Thane'* with *'Lord'*. While not strictly in keeping with the Scottish heritage of the play, the word *'Lord'* is more readily understandable by readers of all nations.

To aid in understanding speeches and for learning lines, where possible, speeches by any character are not broken over two pages unless they have a natural break. As a result of this, gaps will be noticeable at the bottom of pages where the next speech will not fully fit onto the page. This was intentional. A speech can not be fully appreciated if one has to turn the page back and forth when studying or learning lines.

The joy of having a highly accurate English translation is that it can be translated into other languages more readily, foreign language versions of the modern text will be available soon..

Also available soon, a wonderful, innovative app, a huge undertaking and the very first of its kind, which will include full, newly filmed interactive versions of Shakespeare's plays in both original and modern English.

For further info

www.InteractiveShakespeare.com

www.facebook.com/InteractiveShakespeare

@iShakes1 on Twitter

Historical Notes

Shakespeare's *Macbeth* is based on *Holinshed's Chronicles* (1577) which is not historically accurate. Shakespeare then introduced more inaccuracies for dramatic effect and because the play was to be first performed before *King James I* and the *King of Denmark*.

The real *Macbeth*, nicknamed *Rí Deircc*, "The Red King", lived from 1005 – 1057 and was King of Alba (or King of Scots) from 1040 until his death, though he ruled over only a portion of present-day Scotland.

All we know of *Macbeth's* early life is that he was the son of *Findláech of Moray* and may have been a grandson of *Malcolm II*. He became *Mormaer of Moray*, equivalent to a lord, in 1032, probably having killed the previous mormaer, *Gille Coemgáin*, whose widow, *Gruoch*, *Macbeth* married. *Lady Macbeth* had a son, *Lulach*, by her previous husband who then became Macbeth's stepson, though, as in Shakespeare's *Macbeth*, they had no children together.

In 1040, the King of Alba, *Duncan I*, invaded Moray and was killed by *Macbeth's* army. *Macbeth* succeeded him as king, and was highly respected during his 17-year reign which was mostly peaceful, with the exception of an English invasion by *Siward, Earl of Northumbria*, which had the backing of the English king, *Edward the Confessor*, in 1054. *Macbeth* was killed at the Battle of Lumphanan in 1057, fighting the army of the future *King Malcolm III*. He was buried on Iona, the traditional resting place of Scottish kings.

Macbeth was succeeded by his stepson, *Lulach*, who ruled only a few months before also being killed by *Malcolm III* whose descendants would rule Scotland until the late 13th century.

One reason for Shakespeare's unflattering version of *Macbeth* is that *King James* was descended from *Malcolm III* via the House of Bruce and his own House of Stuart, whereas *Macbeth's* line died out with the death of *Lulach*. *King James* also believed he was descended from *Banquo* through *Walter Stuart*, 6th High Steward of Scotland.

The *Tragedy of Macbeth* was first performed on August 7, 1606, at Hampton Court Palace before *King James I* and *King Christian IV* of Denmark. It portrays the results of physical and psychological corruption when pursuing power for its own sake. It was first published in the *Folio* of 1623, and is notably Shakespeare's shortest tragedy by a long way, being over a thousand lines shorter than *Othello* and *King Lear*, and about half the length of *Hamlet*. This has led scholars to believe that it is based perhaps on a heavily cut prompt-book. In other Shakespearean plays the later *Quarto* version was usually longer than the early *Folio* version. *Macbeth* was included in the *First Folio*, but has no *Quarto* version, which would probably have been longer than the *Folio* version. This may explain the fast pace of the first act, and the lack of depth of the main characters apart from *Macbeth*.

There are three main sources for the play, principally *Holinshed's Chronicles* (1587), an inaccurate history of England, Scotland and Ireland. Shakespeare would heavily modify this history in his play. In *Chronicles*, *Donwald* finds several of his family put to death by *King Duff* for his involvement with witches. After pressure from his wife, he and four of his servants kill *King Duff* in his own house. The new *King Duncan's* poor rule alienates *Macbeth*, so he and *Banquo* meet the three witches who make the same prophecies as in Shakespeare's version. *Macbeth* and *Banquo*, with *Lady Macbeth's* encouragement, murder *King Duncan*. *Macbeth* reigns for ten years before being overthrown by *Macduff* and *Malcolm*. Although the similarities are clear, some scholars believe that George Buchanan's *'Rerum Scoticarum Historia'* is closer to Shakespeare's *Macbeth* even though Buchanan's work was available only in Latin at the time.

Shakespeare made another important change. In *Chronicles*, *Banquo* is an accomplice in *Macbeth's* murder of *King Duncan*, and plays an important part in ensuring that *Macbeth*, not *Malcolm*, takes the throne. In Shakespeare's day, *Banquo* was thought to be an ancestor of the Stuart King, *James I*. In more recent years it has been established that the Stuarts are actually descended from a Breton family which migrated to Scotland slightly later than *Macbeth's* time, not from *Banquo*.

The first mention of *Banquo*, the *Weird Sisters*, and *Lady Macbeth* was in 1527 by Hector Boece in *'Historia Gentis Scotorum'* (History of the Scottish People) which was an attempt to damage the reputation of *Macbeth* to further the claim of the House of Stuart to the Scottish throne. *Banquo* was shown as an ancestor of the Stuart kings of Scotland, adding in a prophecy that the descendants of *Banquo* would be the future kings of Scotland while the *Weird Sisters* helped *King Macbeth* gain the throne with witchcraft. *Macbeth's* wife, was portrayed as power-hungry and ambitious which further showed *Macbeth* lacked a proper claim to the throne, and only obtained it because his wife pushed him. Holinshed copied Boece's version of *Macbeth's* reign in his *Chronicles*.

No other version of *Macbeth* had him kill the king in his own castle. Shakespeare probably added to the evil of *Macbeth's* crime by violating his hospitality, as it was generally believed at the time that *Duncan* was killed in an ambush at Inverness, not in a castle.

The second source for the play is from the *'Daemonologie of King James'* published in 1597 which included a news pamphlet titled *'Newes from Scotland'* which recorded the famous North Berwick Witch Trials of 1590. Published just a few years before *Macbeth* and was a result of *James I's* obsessive interest in witchcraft. The trials took place in Scotland, with the accused witches confessing to rituals similar to the three witches in *Macbeth*. The witches in the trial confessed to the use of witchcraft to raise a tempest and sabotage the boat of *King James* and his queen during their return trip from Denmark. One ship with *King James'* fleet sank in the storm.

The third source is the *Gunpowder Plot* of 1605, and the execution of *Father Henry Garnett* for his alleged involvement in the *Gunpowder Plot*. He refused to give direct answers to questions under oath based on the beliefs of the Jesuit practice of equivocation. Shakespeare emphasised *James's* belief that equivocation was a wicked practice, which reflected the wickedness of the Catholic Church. When arrested, *Garnett* had in his possession *A Treatise on Equivocation.*

In the theatre world, it is believed that the play is cursed, and the title of the play should never be spoken aloud, instead calling it *"The Scottish Play"*, though there is no single reason this should be so.

Shakespeare's use of pre-existing material was not considered a lack of originality. In Elizabethan times copyright law did not exist, copying whole passages of text was frequently practiced and not considered theft as it is today. Nowadays, stage and movie productions are frequently 'adaptations' from other sources, the only difference being the need to obtain permission or rights to do so, unless the work is out of copyright.

The real skill Shakespeare displays is in how he adapts his sources in new ways, displaying a remarkable understanding of human psyche and emotion, and including a talent at building characters, adding characters for effect, dramatic pacing, tension building, interspersed by short bouts of relief before building the tension even further, and above all of course, his extraordinary ability to use and miss-use language to his and dramatic, bawdy or playful advantage.

It has been said Shakespeare almost wrote screenplays, predating modern cinema by over 400 years, however you view it, he wrote a powerful story and understood how to play on human emotions and weaknesses.

This play was written during the reign of James I (of England, James VI of Scotland – the first monarch to rule both countries). As Shakespeare often refers to the reigning monarch in his plays indirectly and often performed his plays before the monarch this is useful to know.

DRAMATIS PERSONAE

KING DUNCAN,   King of Scotland

Prince MALCOLM,   } Sons of
Prince DONALBAIN,   } the King

MACBETH,   } Generals of
BANQUO,   } the King's army

LADY MACBETH,   Wife to Macbeth

FLEANCE,   Son to Banquo

MACDUFF,
LENNOX,
ROSS,   Noblemen
CAITHNESS,   of Scotland
ANGUS,
MENTEITH,

LADY MACDUFF,   Wife to Macduff
BOY,   Son to Macduff

SIWARD,   Earl of Northumberland, general
                         of the English forces.
YOUNG SIWARD,   His son

SEYTON,   An officer attending Macbeth

A CAPTAIN,   Serving under King Duncan

Dramatis Personae continued;

An ENGLISH DOCTOR,
A SCOTTISH DOCTOR,   Attending on Lady Macbeth
A WAITING-GENTLEWOMAN,   Attending on Lady Macbeth
A PORTER.
An OLD MAN.
A SOLDIER.

1st MURDERER,
2nd MURDERER,
3rd MURDERER.

HECATE,   Queen of the Witches
1st WITCH,
2nd WITCH,
3rd WITCH.
Three other WITCHES.

The GHOST OF BANQUO.
1st APPARITION,   An Armoured Head
2nd APPARITION,   A Bloody Child
3rd APPARITION,   A Crowned Child

EIGHT KINGS,   A Show of Eight Apparitions.

Lords, Attendants, Trumpeters, Drummers, Torch-bearers,
Standard Bearers, Soldiers, Messengers, Serving Staff.

SCENE: SCOTLAND; ENGLAND

CONTENTS

ACT I

ACT I SCENE I
A Deserted Clearing on a Stormy Morning 18
ACT I SCENE II
A Military Camp near Forres, Scotland 20
ACT I SCENE III
A Deserted Heath 25
ACT I SCENE IV
The King's Palace at Forres 36
ACT I SCENE V
Macbeth's Castle. The Drawing Room 41
Macbeth's Castle. Later that day 44
ACT I SCENE VI
Outside Macbeth's Castle 47
ACT I SCENE VII
i Macbeth's Castle. Outside the Great Hall. 50
ii Inside the Great Hall 51
iii Outside the Great Hall 52

ACT II

ACT II SCENE I
The Castle Courtyard. Night 58
ACT II SCENE II
Castle Bedchamber. Night 65
ACT II SCENE III
The Castle Main Gate at Dawn 74
ACT II SCENE IV
Macbeth's Castle Later That Morning 86

ACT III

ACT III SCENE I
The King's Palace. Banquo's Quarters 90
ACT III SCENE II
King's Palace at Forres. Later On 98
ACT III SCENE III
Some Distance from the Palace. Dusk 101
ACT III SCENE IV
The Hall of the Palace. A Banquet 104
ACT III SCENE V
A Heath 115
ACT III SCENE VI
The King's Palace at Forres 117

ACT IV

ACT IV SCENE I

    i Witches' Lair at Acheron. Night. 122

    ii Outside the Royal Palace. Night..123

    iii Acheron. Witches' Lair. Night. 123

    iv Outside the Witches Lair. Just Before Sunrise.......................................125

    v Inside the Witches' Lair...126

    vi A Heath next to A Rocky Outcrop. Dawn. 134

    vii Inside the Witches' Lair. Dawn. 134

ACT IV SCENE II

    Macduff's Castle, Fife. 136

ACT IV SCENE III

    The English King's Palace Grounds 143

ACT V

ACT V SCENE I

    A Bedchamber in Castle Dunsinane 156

ACT V SCENE II

    A Secret Place near Dunsinane 162

ACT V SCENE III

    A Court of Castle Dunsinane...164

ACT V SCENE IV

    The Countryside near Birnam Wood 170

ACT V SCENE V

    A Court of Castle Dunsinane...172

ACT V SCENE VI

    The Castle Gate at Dunsinane 176

ACT V SCENE VII

    Large Hall in the Castle 177

    A Court of the Castle 178

ACT V SCENE VIII

    Castle Banquetting Hall 180

ACT V SCENE IX

    The Castle Courtyard 183

ACT I

SCOTLAND
ELEVENTH CENTURY A.D.

GOOD IS EVIL, AND EVIL IS GOOD

ACT I

ACT I SCENE I

A Deserted Clearing on a Stormy Morning.

Thunder, lightning and a fierce wind rage.

Three ugly, bearded witches meet at the edge of a clearing.

> *Note: To show the characters are comedic, mad or evil, Shakespeare writes their lines in prose rather than the usual blank verse – a form of poetry which doesn't rhyme except for dramatic effect. Shakespeare also used rhyme for certain characters, such as the witches, and the type of rhyme would vary depending on the character who spoke it. In Macbeth, characters who speak in rhyme are typically evil.*
>
> *Rhymed lines are in italics.*

WITCH 1
When shall we three meet again?
In thunder, lightning, or in rain?

WITCH 2
When the hurly-burly's done,
When the battle's lost and won.

FIRST WITCH
When shall we three meet again?
In thunder, lightning, or in rain?

SECOND WITCH
When the hurlyburly's done;
When the battle's lost and won.

> *Note: 'Hurly-burly' - loud, boisterous behaviour.*
> *'Lost and won' - battle ended; playing on a theme of opposites. One side lost, one side won.*
> *'Ere the set of sun' - it will happen today.*

WITCH 3
Before the setting of the sun.

WITCH 1
Where to meet?

WITCH 2
Upon the heath.

WITCH 3
There to meet Macbeth.

THIRD WITCH
That will be ere the set of sun.

FIRST WITCH
Where the place?

SECOND WITCH
Upon the heath.

THIRD WITCH
There to meet with Macbeth.

> *Note: 'Heath' was pronounced 'heth' in Shakespeare's time so would have rhymed with 'Macbeth' in the line which followed it.*

Act I Scene I. A Deserted Clearing.

A CAT (WITCH 1'S FAMILIAR) CALLS A WEIRD WARNING CRY.

| **WITCH 1** | FIRST WITCH |
| I'm coming, old Moggins! | I come, Graymalkin. |

A TOAD CROAKS AS IF TO ALSO NOTIFY THE WITCHES.

Note: 'Puddock' was a Scottish word for toad. In Scottish folklore 'Greymalkin' was a fairy cat found in the highlands. 'Moggie' is a cat of mixed pedigree and 'moggins' is an affectionate term for any cat nowadays.

WITCH 2	SECOND WITCH
(*cocking her head, listening*)	Paddock calls.
Paddock calls.	

| **WITCH 3** | THIRD WITCH |
| It will be soon! | Anon! |

THEY LAUGH WICKEDLY AND RAISE ARMS, CHANTING TOGETHER.

WITCHES	ALL
Good is evil, and evil is good.	*Fair is foul, and foul is fair.*
Fly us through mist and filthy fog!	*Hover through the fog and filthy air.*

A THICK MIST ROLLS IN AND THEY VANISH INTO THIN AIR.

Note: The witches in Macbeth have been forever embedded into our culture. We still refer back to Shakespeare's version every year on Halloween. Shakespeare's version of witches was a mixture of the English and Scottish ideas of witches and witchcraft. Common beliefs of the time were that witches could fly, cast spells, place curses, cause plagues, and had an evil spirit accompany them which took the appearance of an animal, often a cat, and this was known as the witch's 'familiar', short for 'familiar spirit'. A Scottish word for a toad is 'puddock'.

Throughout the play there runs a theme of opposites. Prominently; good and evil.

<u>Important Note:</u> *Scholars believe that Macbeth as we know it is based perhaps on a heavily cut prompt-book, concentrating on the main action of the play only, which is why the play is so much shorter than the other tragedies. It was not included in the earliest printings of his works, so we have nothing to compare it with as we have with other plays of his. This may explain the fast pace of the first act, and the lack of depth of the main characters apart from Macbeth. It may also explain the missing details and time jumps, and the inserted musical interludes written by another person or persons.*

ACT I SCENE II

A MILITARY CAMP NEAR FORRES, SCOTLAND.

> Note: The wording and phrasing in this scene is particularly difficult to understand at first read, leading to some scholars suggesting this was not the work of Shakespeare. It is likely that it has been edited down from the original wording but there is no proof it is not Shakespeare's work. Once the modern translation has been read the original wording will be easier to follow. Some editions call the soldier 'Sergeant' some call him 'Captain' - both were used here.

KING DUNCAN OF SCOTLAND RIDES TOWARDS A BATTLEFIELD WITH HIS SONS, MALCOLM AND DONALBAIN, AND THE NOBLEMAN LORD LENNOX.

ARRIVING AT A MILITARY CAMP THEY COME ACROSS A WOUNDED SOLDIER.

THE GROUP STOP BY HIS SIDE.

KING DUNCAN
Who is that bloodied man? Judging by his wounds, he can deliver fresh news of the rebellion.

PRINCE MALCOLM
It's the Captain, father, who fought so courageously to prevent my capture.
(to Captain) Greetings, brave friend! Inform the King how the skirmish fared when you left it.

ARMY CAPTAIN
(in pain from his wounds) Your Majesty... There was little between us, two sides like tired swimmers clinging together, dragging each other down. But the merciless, Macdonwald, - truly a vile traitor, judging by the dregs of humanity that swarm to him - was backed by foot soldiers and heavily armed mercenaries from the western isles.

DUNCAN
What bloody man is that? He can report,
As seemeth by his plight, of the revolt
The newest state.

MALCOLM
This is the sergeant,
Who, like a good and hardy soldier fought
'Gainst my captivity. Hail, brave friend!
Say to the King the knowledge of the broil
As thou didst leave it.

SERGEANT:
(in pain from his wounds)
Doubtful it stood,
As two spent swimmers that do cling together
And choke their art. The merciless Macdonwald—
Worthy to be a rebel, for to that
The multiplying villainies of nature
Do swarm upon him—from the western isles
Of kerns and gallowglasses is supplied;

> Note: The 'Western Isles' are the Outer Hebrides, a chain of islands off the west coast of Scotland, however it was likely to have been a reference to Ireland as 'kerns' were lightly armed foot soldiers from Ireland and 'gallowglasses' were ruthless mercenaries in the service of Irish tribal chieftains.

ARMY CAPTAIN (CONT'D)

For a while, fortune smiled like a rebel's whore in his favour. But 'twas not enough, no, for the brave Macbeth - and well he deserves that title - spitting in the face of fortune, brandishing his steaming, bloodied sword like the courageous hero of valour, carved his way through till he faced that low-life scum, Macdonwald. Then without so much as a by-your-leave, Macbeth had opened him from belly to jaw, and fixed his head high above our battle line for all to see.

SERGEANT:

And fortune, on his damned quarrel smiling,
Show'd like a rebel's whore, but all's too weak;
For brave Macbeth—well he deserves that name—
Disdaining fortune, with his brandish'd steel,
Which smoked with bloody execution,
Like valor's minion carved out his passage
Till he faced the slave,
Which ne'er shook hands, nor bade farewell to
  him,
Till he unseam'd him from the nave to the chaps,
And fix'd his head upon our battlements.

Note: What Macbeth does here is significant to the play's ending. The defeated leader would be beheaded and his head displayed impaled on a pike (a weapon) high for all to see. It served two purposes, one was for the victor to gloat, the other was for the losing side's men to see they had lost and "lay down their arms" (surrender or flee). Similarly, traitor's heads were displayed impaled on pikes on the battlements of London Bridge for all to see.

KING DUNCAN

Oh my valiant cousin, Macbeth! Worthy nobleman.

DUNCAN

O valiant cousin! Worthy gentleman!

Note: In Shakespeare's time 'cousin' meant 'relative', though Duncan and Macbeth were actual first cousins in real life, sharing the same grandfather.

ARMY CAPTAIN

And as, "*the calm before the storm is but short respite 'ere the dire thunders break*", from that same source where comforting news had sprung forth, discomforting news was brewing. - Listen, King of Scotland, and take note! No sooner had our brave men, newly fortified in their victory, forced those footloose rebels to their heels, than the Viking King - now with restocked arms and fresh supplies of men - saw his opportunity and launched a fresh assault.

SERGEANT

As whence the sun 'gins his reflection
Shipwrecking storms and direful thunders break,
So from that spring whence comfort seem'd to
  come
Discomfort swells. Mark, King of Scotland, mark:
No sooner justice had, with valor arm'd,
Compell'd these skipping kerns to trust their
  heels,
But the Norweyan lord, surveying vantage,
With furbish'd arms and new supplies of men,
Began a fresh assault.

KING DUNCAN

(*shocked*) Were our Generals, Macbeth and Banquo, not overwhelmed by this?

DUNCAN

Dismay'd not this
Our captains, Macbeth and Banquo?

ARMY CAPTAIN
(*jokingly, but coughing with pain*) Yes...
(*he smiles*) like lions overrun by hares, or eagles by sparrows.

SERGEANT
Yes,
As sparrows eagles, or the hare the lion.

AT HIS STATEMENT THE ENTOURAGE LAUGH.

ARMY CAPTAIN (CON'T)
I swear they were like cannons loaded with double charges. Heroically they doubled and redoubled their strikes against their foe, as if they planned to bathe in blood or re-enact the fields of dead at Calvary, I know not which...

SERGEANT
If I say sooth, I must report they were
As cannons overcharged with double cracks,
So they doubly redoubled strokes upon the foe.
Except they meant to bathe in reeking wounds,
Or memorize another Golgotha,
I cannot tell —

COUGHING UP BLOOD, THE CAPTAIN STRUGGLES TO CARRY ON.

Note: Golgotha (which means 'place of skulls') was the site of mass crucifixions on the hill of Calvary outside Jerusalem, including that of Jesus Christ.

ARMY CAPTAIN (CONT'D)
I feel faint, my wounds cry out for attention.

SERGEANT
But I am faint; my gashes cry for help.

KING DUNCAN
Your words do you proud, as do your wounds. Both smack of honour.

DUNCAN
So well thy words become thee as thy wounds;
They smack of honor both.

CAPTAIN GROANS LOUDLY AND SLUMPS, BECOMING DELIRIOUS.

KING DUNCAN (CON'T)
Call surgeons, quickly!

DUNCAN
Go get him surgeons.

Note: In Shakespeare's time pain killers and antibiotics didn't exist. A surgeon would amputate a damaged limb with a saw while the man was conscious. The man would likely die from infection or shock.

If a patient was lucky, he would be given strong alcohol to alleviate the shock and the pain to some extent. At sea there was an old saying "four measures of ship's grog is sufficient to amputate a limb". Grog was rum mixed with water, the rum on board ship was very high in alcohol as less was required to be carried and have the same alcoholic effect.

TWO HORSES FAST APPROACH AND DISTRACT THE ROYAL ENTOURAGE.

KING DUNCAN (CON'T)
Who comes there?

DUNCAN
Who comes here?

Act I Scene II. A Military Camp.

> Note: The cry of "Halt. Who comes there?" can be heard every day at the Tower of London during the Ceremony of the Keys, the same wording used for 700 years.

PRINCE MALCOLM	MALCOLM
It's the honourable Lord of Ross, father.	The worthy Thane of Ross.
LORD LENNOX	LENNOX
And by the look in his eyes, a man in all haste to give us some alarming news	What a haste looks through his eyes! So should he look that seems to speak things strange.

LORD ROSS AND LORD ANGUS, TWO LOYAL NOBLEMEN, RIDE UP.

LORD ROSS	ROSS
(*riding up, rushed*) God save the King!	God save the King!
KING DUNCAN	DUNCAN
From where do you come, noble Lord?	Whence cam'st thou, worthy Thane?
LORD ROSS	ROSS
(*Rushing to get the news out*) From Fife, your majesty, where the Viking banners fan our people with their cold terror. There, the King of Norway himself, with terrible numbers of men, aided by that treacherous traitor, the Lord of Cawdor, launched a terrible onslaught. - That was, until that god of war himself, Macbeth, in battle-scarred armour, confronted him with a taste of his own medicine. Point to point, hand to hand, he cut his high spirits down to size. And to conclude... The victory was ours!	From Fife, great King, Where the Norweyan banners flout the sky And fan our people cold. Norway himself, with terrible numbers, Assisted by that most disloyal traitor The Thane of Cawdor, began a dismal conflict, Till that Bellona's bridegroom, lapp'd in proof, Confronted him with self-comparisons, Point against point rebellious, arm 'gainst arm, Curbing his lavish spirit; and, to conclude, The victory fell on us.

ALL LAUGH AND CHEER AT THE NEWS.

KING DUNCAN	DUNCAN
Great news!	Great happiness!

LORD ROSS THROWS THE ROYAL SEAL OF CAWDOR TO PRINCE MALCOLM WHO CATCHES IT AND STUDIES IT. UPON IT IS ENGRAVED 'CAWDOR' AND A COAT OF ARMS. HE HANDS IT TO HIS FATHER, THE KING.

LORD ROSS	ROSS
Now King Sweno of Norway seeks a truce. We have refused him permission to bury his men on the holy isle of Inchcolm until he pays us ten thousand pounds compensation.	That now Sweno, the Norways' king, craves composition; Nor would we deign him burial of his men Till he disbursed, at Saint Colme's Inch, Ten thousand dollars to our general use.

KING DUNCAN	DUNCAN
The Lord of Cawdor shall deceive us with his treachery no longer. *Now go at once and put Cawdor to death, Present his former title to Macbeth.*	No more that Thane of Cawdor shall deceive *Our bosom interest. Go pronounce his present death, And with his former title greet Macbeth.*

THE KING HANDS THE SEAL BACK TO PRINCE MALCOLM,
WHO IN TURN HANDS IT BACK TO LORD ROSS

LORD ROSS	ROSS
I'll see it is done.	*I'll see it done.*
KING DUNCAN	**DUNCAN**
What he has lost, noble Macbeth has won.	*What he hath lost, noble Macbeth hath won.*

ROSS AND ANGUS DEPART AT SPEED TO DELIVER THE NEWS TO MACBETH.

Note: Rhyming couplets here signify the end of a scene. In Shakespeare's day there were no curtains, no lights and mostly static scenery – so scene changes were not so obvious. The rhyming lines, though not strictly necessary, are included to maintain the feel of the original.

Audiences were conditioned to hear the rhyme and knew the significance. The remainder of the play would be mostly written in blank verse, which is not rhymed, so the contrast was apparent.

Shakespeare also used rhyme for certain characters, such as the witches, and the type of rhyme would vary depending on the character who spoke it. In Macbeth, characters who speak in rhyme are typically evil.

Note: The title 'Thane' has been replaced in this translation with 'Lord'. While not strictly in keeping with the Scottish heritage of the play, the word 'Lord' is more readily understandable by present day readers of all nations.

Important Note: The stage directions (between main text in capital letters) are included purely as the author's guide to understand the script better. Any director staging the play would have their own interpretation of the play and decide their own directions. These directions are not those of Shakespeare. You can change these directions to your own choosing or ignore them completely. For exam purposes these should be only regarded as guidance to the dialogue and for accuracy should not be quoted in any studies or examinations.

ACT I SCENE III

A DESERTED HEATH.

THUNDER AND LIGHTNING.

THE THREE WITCHES ARE GATHERED TOGETHER
ON A HEATH ARAUND AN OPEN FIRE.

WITCH 1
Where have you been, sister?

WITCH 2
Killing swine.

WITCH 3
And sister, where were you?

WITCH 1
A sailor's wife had chestnuts in her lap,
And munched and munched and munched.
'Give me one!' said I
'Be gone, you witch!' the bloated slut did cry.
Her husband's sailed to Aleppo, Captain of the 'Tiger'.
But in a sieve, I'll to it sail,
And like a rat without a tail,
I'll do him, do him, do him!

FIRST WITCH
Where hast thou been, sister?

SECOND WITCH
Killing swine.

THIRD WITCH
Sister, where thou?

FIRST WITCH
A sailor's wife had chestnuts in her lap,
And mounch'd, and mounch'd, and mounch'd.
"Give me," quoth I.
"Aroint thee, witch!" the rump-fed ronyon cries.
Her husband's to Aleppo gone, master o' the Tiger;
But in a sieve I'll thither sail,
And, like a rat without a tail,
I'll do, I'll do, and I'll do.

Note: 'Do him' is a bawdy innuendo. The symbolism of a rat without a tail is a naked, wretched human. Witches were thought to cast spells on people, rather like hypnotising or drugging them and having their evil, lusty way with them. Here it is used with the additional double meaning of doing him harm.

The Tiger was a ship which sailed to Aleppo on 5th Dec 1604 and arrived back after fearful experiences on 27th June 1606 after 568 days - exactly the seven nights times nine times nine, and importantly, two months before this play was first staged.

There is good reason for including the witches and their effect on ships. King James published Daemonologie in 1597 which included details of the famous North Berwick Witch Trials of 1590. It was published a few years before Macbeth was first performed in front of King James who was obsessively interested in witchcraft. The witches involved were said to have conducted rituals with the same mannerisms as the three witches here. The witches in the trial confessed to using witchcraft to raise a tempest and sabotage the ship King James and his Queen were on during their return trip from Denmark. One ship sailing with King James' fleet sank in the storm.

WITCH 2

I'll give you a wind.

WITCH 1

You're kind.

WITCH 3

  And I another.

WITCH 1

I myself have all the others,
And the ports to which they blow,
From all directions that they know
Upon the sailor's chart.
I will drain him dry as hay,
He will not sleep night or day.
With drooping lids upon his eyes,
He'll live but barely be alive.
Through weary weeks, nine times nine,
He shall weaken, starve and pine.
Though his ship will not be lost,
It shall e'er be tempest tossed...
- Look what I have...

WITCH 2

Show me, Show me!

WITCH 1

Here I have a sailor's thumb,
Ripped off as homeward he did come.

A VIOLENT THUNDER CRACK.

WITCH 3

A drum, a drum!
Macbeth does come.

SECOND WITCH

I'll give thee a wind.

FIRST WITCH

Thou'rt kind.

THIRD WITCH

  And I another.

FIRST WITCH

I myself have all the other,
And the very ports they blow,
All the quarters that they know
I' the shipman's card.
I will drain him dry as hay:
Sleep shall neither night nor day
Hang upon his penthouse lid;
He shall live a man forbid.
Weary se'n nights nine times nine
Shall he dwindle, peak, and pine;
Though his bark cannot be lost,
Yet it shall be tempest-tost.
Look what I have.

SECOND WITCH

Show me, show me.

FIRST WITCH

Here I have a pilot's thumb,
Wrack'd as homeward he did come.

THIRD WITCH

A drum, a drum!
Macbeth doth come.

HOLDING HANDS THEY CIRCLE THE FIRE, CHANTING TOGETHER.

Note: Two senior military figures such as Macbeth and Banquo would have been accompanied by attendants and a military guard. Attendants would bang a drum to keep time as they marched onto stage. Realistically they would have been riding horses, but they could not be used on stage. Drums were also used to announce arrival of someone royal or high up and for various sound effects. As there is no mention of other personnel, thunder makes a convenient replacement.

Thunder sound effect was created by rolling a cannon ball down a metal chute.

Act I Scene III. A Deserted Heath.

WITCHES

We Witch Sisters, hand in hand,
Travellers of the sea and land,
Now do go around, around.
Thrice to yours and thrice to mine,
And thrice again, to make it nine.
Enough! The spell is done.

ALL

The weird sisters, hand in hand,
Posters of the sea and land,
Thus do go about, about:
Thrice to thine, and thrice to mine,
And thrice again, to make up nine.
Peace! The charm's wound up.

RAISING THEIR ARMS, THE FIRE ERUPTS FLAME AND SMOKE.

THUNDER CRACKS AGAIN. IT STARTS TO RAIN HEAVILY.

MACBETH AND BANQUO, BOTH BLOODIED, BATTERED, AND TRIUMPHANT,
RIDE ONTO THE SAME OPEN HEATH ON WAR HORSES.

AS THEY NEAR THE EDGE OF THE HEATH WHERE THERE IS A
ROCKY OUTCROP THE HORSES SPOOK AND STOP.

MACBETH

I've not seen a day like it, Banquo. Such evil weather after such good fortune.

MACBETH

So foul and fair a day I have not seen.

BANQUO LOOKS UP AT THE SKY, WISHING THE JOURNEY TO BE
OVER SOON, TO BE OUT OF THE RAIN AND CELEBRATING.

BANQUO

How much farther to Forres, Macbeth?

BANQUO

How far is't call'd to Forres?

Note: Forres is where the King's royal palace is located.

BANQUO THEN NOTICES THE WITCHES AND PULLS HIS RELUCTANT
HORSE OVER TO THEM. THE HORSE REACTS WITH FEAR.

BANQUO (CON'T)

Whoa. (*calming his horse*)
What are these creatures? So withered, and wild of attire. Like beings not of this earth, though apparently on it.

BANQUO

What are these
So wither'd, and so wild in their attire,
That look not like the inhabitants o' the earth,
And yet are on't?

MACBETH JOINS BANQUO.

THE WITCHES RAISE THEIR ARMS AND THE RAIN MAGICALLY CLEARS.

BANQUO (CON'T)

(*to witches*) Are you alive? Or are you spirits men may question?

BANQUO

Live you? or are you aught
That man may question?

27

THE WITCHES LOOK UP AT BANQUO AND EACH PUT A GNARLED FINGER TO
THEIR SHRIVELLED LIPS. IT IS NOT BANQUO THEY WISH TO TALK TO.

BANQUO (CON'T)	BANQUO
They seem to understand me, look, they put their craggy fingers to their shrivelled lips.	You seem to understand me, By each at once her choppy finger laying Upon her skinny lips.

BANQUO EXAMINES THEM, CONFUSED.

BANQUO (CON'T)	BANQUO
You look like women, yet your beards suggest otherwise.	You should be women, And yet your beards forbid me to interpret That you are so.
MACBETH	**MACBETH**
Speak, if you can. Who are you?	Speak, if you can. What are you?

THE WITCHES TURN THEIR GAZE TO MACBETH.

Note: Now that Macbeth has spoken with them they can reply to him. It was believed
supernatural beings could only speak if they had been spoken to first.

WITCH 1	FIRST WITCH
All praise, Macbeth! Praise be to you, Lord of Glamis!	All hail, Macbeth! hail to thee, Thane of Glamis!

MACBETH AND BANQUO LOOK AT EACH OTHER,
SURPRISED THE WITCH KNEW HIS NAME AND TITLE.

WITCH 2	SECOND WITCH
All praise, Macbeth! Praise be to you, Lord of Cawdor!	All hail, Macbeth! hail to thee, Thane of Cawdor!
WITCH 3	**THIRD WITCH**
All praise, Macbeth! (she points to Macbeth) Who shall be King!	All hail, Macbeth! that shalt be King hereafter!
BANQUO	**BANQUO**
Good sir, why so startled? Are you afraid to hear good things?	Good sir, why do you start, and seem to fear Things that do sound so fair?

Note: Macbeth is taken aback by the prophecy. Banquo is not so taken in by the
Witches, it all sounds too far-fetched. Macbeth's shock may also have been because
he had been plotting before, which may have originally been explored in more detail
in the full length version of Macbeth of which no known copy exists.

BANQUO IS A LITTLE ANNOYED THEY TALK WITH MACBETH BUT NOT HIM.

BANQUO (CON'T)

(*to Witches*) In the name of God, are you spirits, or as mortal as your appearance suggests? You greet my noble friend with his noble title, then predict hope of further titles, one of them so great he is lost in bewilderment. Yet to me you say nothing.

BANQUO

(*to witches*) I' the name of truth,
Are ye fantastical or that indeed
Which outwardly ye show? My noble partner
You greet with present grace and great prediction
Of noble having and of royal hope,
That he seems rapt withal. To me you speak not.

THE WITCHES TURN TO BANQUO BUT SAY NOTHING.

BANQUO (CON'T)

If you truly can look into the seeds of time, and say which seed will grow, and which will not, then tell me my fortune. I ask for no kindness, nor do I fear your words.

BANQUO

If you can look into the seeds of time,
And say which grain will grow and which will not,
Speak then to me, who neither beg nor fear
Your favors nor your hate.

THE WITCHES FINALLY ANSWER BANQUO.

WITCH 1

Praise!

FIRST WITCH

Hail!

WITCH 2

Praise!

SECOND WITCH

Hail!

WITCH 3

Praise!

THIRD WITCH

Hail!

WITCH 1

Lesser than Macbeth you will be... And yet, greater.

FIRST WITCH

Lesser than Macbeth, and greater.

WITCH 2

Not so happy... And yet, much happier.

SECOND WITCH

Not so happy, yet much happier.

WITCH 3

You will sire kings, though you'll not be one. So all praise Macbeth and Banquo!

THIRD WITCH

Thou shalt get kings, though thou be none.
So all hail, Macbeth and Banquo!

WITCH 1

Banquo and Macbeth, all praise!

FIRST WITCH

Banquo and Macbeth, all hail!

THE WITCHES TURN AND BEGIN TO WALK AWAY.
MACBETH MAKES AFTER THEM, CALLING AFTER THEM.

Note: The witches are vague with their answers to Banquo, unlike with Macbeth. It was falsely believed at the time that the royal house of Stuart, which included James, who the play was written and first performed for, began with Banquo's son, Fleance.

MACBETH

Wait, you've not explained yourselves! Tell me more! I am Lord of Glamis by my father's death, but how of Cawdor? The Lord of Cawdor lives a healthy, prosperous life. And to be King is even more preposterous than the title of Cawdor! Tell me how you came by such knowledge, and why, upon this God-forsaken heath, you stop us with such prophetic words?

MACBETH

Stay, you imperfect speakers, tell me more.
By Sinel's death I know I am Thane of Glamis;
But how of Cawdor? The Thane of Cawdor lives,
A prosperous gentleman; and to be King
Stands not within the prospect of belief,
No more than to be Cawdor. Say from whence
You owe this strange intelligence, or why
Upon this blasted heath you stop our way
With such prophetic greeting?

> Note: Shakespeare took the name 'Sinel' from Holinshed's Chronicles, which was not historically accurate. The real Macbeth, born in 1005, had a father named Findlaech, who was the ruler of Moray in Northern Scotland.

A SUDDEN THICK MIST ROLLS OVER THE CACKLING WITCHES, OBSCURING THEM FROM VIEW.

THE WIND GETS LOUDER AS THE WITCHES VANISH, SUCKING THE MIST WITH THEM INTO A VACUUM.

MACBETH (CON'T)

Wait! Speak, I order you!

MACBETH

Speak, I charge you.

THE MIST CLEARS TO REVEAL THE WITCHES HAVE VANISHED.

MACBETH RIDES OVER TO EXAMINE A ROCK FORMATION TOWARDS WHICH THE MIST HAD HEADED. THERE IS NO SIGN OF THE WITCHES.

BANQUO

It seems the earth has bubbles like water does, and these are some of them. Where did they vanish to?

BANQUO

The earth hath bubbles as the water has,
And these are of them. Whither are they vanish'd?

MACBETH

Into the air, Banquo. They seemed solid, but melted like breath in the wind. If only they'd stayed longer.

MACBETH

Into the air, and what seem'd corporal melted
As breath into the wind. Would they had stay'd!

BANQUO

Were they really there? Or have we eaten a poisonous root and lost our minds?

BANQUO

Were such things here as we do speak about?
Or have we eaten on the insane root
That takes the reason prisoner?

> Note: Insane root - a root believed in medieval times to cause madness in those eating it and usually identified with either henbane or hemlock.

MACBETH RIDES SLOWLY BACK TOWARDS BANQUO, DEEP IN THOUGHT, HE HAS TAKEN THE WITCHES PROPHECY FAR MORE SERIOUSLY THAN BANQUO.

Act I Scene III. A Deserted Heath.

MACBETH	MACBETH
Your children will be kings...	Your children shall be kings.
BANQUO	**BANQUO**
...you will be King...	You shall be King.
MACBETH	**MACBETH**
And Lord of Cawdor too, didn't they say?	And Thane of Cawdor too. Went it not so?
BANQUO	**BANQUO**
The self same words they used.	To the self same tune and words.

HORSES APPROACH FROM A DISTANCE. BANQUO TURNS.

BANQUO	BANQUO
Who's this?	Who's here?

MACBETH REACHES FOR HIS SWORD BEFORE RELAXING AS HE RECOGNISES
LORD ROSS AND LORD ANGUS APPROACHING. THEY RIDE UP AND STOP.

ROSS NODS IN GREETING TO EACH MAN THEN ADDRESSES MACBETH DIRECTLY.

LORD ROSS	ROSS
We come from a happy king, Macbeth, at the news of your success.	The King hath happily received, Macbeth, The news of thy success;

MACBETH NODS HAPPILY AT THE WORDS.

LORD ROSS (CON'T)	ROSS
When he heard of your heroic deeds in the fight against the rebels, he was too overcome to sing the praises you deserved, and then overcome with so many praises, words failed him.	and when he reads Thy personal venture in the rebels' fight, His wonders and his praises do contend Which should be thine or his. Silenced with that,

MACBETH REACTS WITH SATISFACTION, LOOKING TOWARDS BANQUO.

LORD ROSS (CON'T)	ROSS
Reviewing the rest of the day's conflict, the king then finds you among the staunch Norwegian lines inflicting carnage all round with no fear for your own life,.	In viewing o'er the rest o' the selfsame day, He finds thee in the stout Norweyan ranks, Nothing afeard of what thyself didst make, Strange images of death.

AGAIN, MACBETH LOOKS PLEASED.

BANQUO IS ANXIOUS TO HEAR OF HIS PRAISES.

31

LORD ROSS (CON'T)	ROSS
As thick as hail report after report came raining down on him, each one singing your praises in defence of his kingdom.	As thick as hail Came post with post, and every one did bear Thy praises in his kingdom's great defense, And pour'd them down before him.
ANGUS	ANGUS
We were sent to convey thanks from our royal master, and to bring you before him in order for him to reward you personally.	We are sent To give thee, from our royal master, thanks; Only to herald thee into his sight, Not pay thee.

ROSS TURNS TO A SADDLE BAG TO RETRIEVE SOMETHING.

LORD ROSS	ROSS
And as proof of a greater honour to come, he ordered we address you...	And for an earnest of a greater honor, He bade me, from him, call thee...

ROSS HOLDS UP THE SEAL OF CAWDOR, OFFERING IT TO MACBETH.

LORD ROSS (CON'T)	ROSS
...'Lord of Cawdor'! To which I add; God save you, most noble Lord, for the title is deservedly yours.	...Thane of Cawdor. In which addition, hail, most worthy Thane, For it is thine.

MACBETH TAKES THE SEAL FROM ROSS, STUDYING IT THOUGHTFULLY.

BANQUO LOOKS VISIBLY SHOCKED.

BANQUO	BANQUO
(shocked) What? Did those devils speak the truth?	What, can the devil speak true?
MACBETH	MACBETH
But the Lord of Cawdor lives. Why do you address me with a borrowed title?	The Thane of Cawdor lives. Why do you dress me In borrow'd robes?
ANGUS	ANGUS
The previous Lord lives, but under sentence of death hangs that life which he will soon deservedly lose.	Who was the Thane lives yet, But under heavy judgement bears that life Which he deserves to lose.

TAKEN ABACK, MACBETH LOOKS TO ANGUS FOR AN EXPLANATION.

ANGUS (CON'T)	ANGUS
Whether he was siding with the Vikings, or secretly aiding that vile rebel, McDonwald -	Whether he was combined With those of Norway, or did line the rebel -

ANGUS SPITS IN DISGUST AT THE NAME

Act I Scene III. A Deserted Heath.

ANGUS (CON'T)

...or attempting to overthrow his country with both, I know not. But high treason, proven and confessed, has sealed his fate.

MACBETH

(*thinking aloud*) Lord of Glamis and now Cawdor, with the greatest title to follow!
(*to Ross & Angus*) I thank you for your trouble, gentlemen.

ANGUS

With hidden help and vantage, or that with both
He labor'd in his country's wrack, I know not;
But treasons capital, confess'd and proved,
Have overthrown him.

MACBETH

(*aside*) Glamis, and Thane of Cawdor!
The greatest is behind.
(*to Ross and Angus*) Thanks for your pains.

ROSS AND ANGUS TURN THEIR HORSES TO LEAD OFF.

MACBETH (CON'T)

(*aside to Banquo*) Don't you hope your children will be kings, Banquo, after those creatures who promised it to you promised the title *'Lord of Cawdor'* to me?

BANQUO

(*aside to Macbeth*) And that same promise may lead you to the crown to sit alongside the title of Cawdor. But I'm uneasy. The disciples of darkness often lead us to harm by tempting us with tales of fortune and offers of petty rewards, before betraying us with their evil consequences.
(*to Ross and Angus*) Friends, a word if I may.

MACBETH

(*aside to Banquo*) Do you not hope your children
   shall be kings,
When those that gave the Thane of Cawdor to me
Promised no less to them?

BANQUO

(*aside to Macbeth*) That, trusted home,
Might yet enkindle you unto the crown,
Besides the Thane of Cawdor. But 'tis strange;
And oftentimes, to win us to our harm,
The instruments of darkness tell us truths,
Win us with honest trifles, to betray's
In deepest consequence —
(*to Ross and Angus*) Cousins, a word, I pray you.

BANQUO HEADS TO ROSS AND ANGUS.

MACBETH REMAINS, DEEP IN THOUGHT.

Note: The speech which follows is Macbeth's first soliloquy. Speaking his thoughts aloud, only he and the audience can hear them.

A soliloquy differs from a monologue or an aside. A monologue is a long speech spoken by only one person. An aside is a short thought or an actor speaking briefly to himself. A soliloquy is a longer speech, with the character speaking his thoughts only to the audience and himself. Unlike a monologue other characters on stage do not hear or react in any way to the words. Only the speaker of the soliloquy and the audience hear the words, which are usually the inner struggles of the speaker's mind.

The following soliloquy is interrupted by interactions of others, but to them it seems that Macbeth is just deep in thought, overwhelmed by the happenings of the day.

MACBETH

(*deep in thought*) Two predictions have come true, as if in joyful prelude to the greatest reward of all; the royal throne! (*aloud*) I thank you, gentlemen.
(*aside*) Is this supernatural intervention good or bad though? If bad, why did it give notice of success to come, starting with an accurate prediction? I am Lord of Cawdor. If good, why does my hair stand on end and my heart pound in my ribs with dread at the thought of it.

MACBETH

(*aside*) Two truths are told,
As happy prologues to the swelling act
Of the imperial theme! — I thank you, gentlemen.
(*aside*) This supernatural soliciting
Cannot be ill, cannot be good. If ill,
Why hath it given me earnest of success,
Commencing in a truth? I am Thane of Cawdor.
If good, why do I yield to that suggestion
Whose horrid image doth unfix my hair
And make my seated heart knock at my ribs,
Against the use of nature?

MACBETH SHUDDERS AT HIS THOUGHTS.

Note: 'Seated heart' means heart at rest, one not being exerted. Seated also means 'established', a part usually in tune with the rest of the body. In this case it is quite obviously not. Clever punning.

MACBETH (CON'T)

My fears are no more than horrible figments of my wild imagination: but the thought of murder, though still a fantasy, so shakes me to the core it stifles my reasoning. I no longer know what is real and what is not.

MACBETH

Present fears
Are less than horrible imaginings:
My thought, whose murder yet is but fantastical,
Shakes so my single state of man that function
Is smother'd in surmise, and nothing is
But what is not.

BANQUO AND THE OTHERS TURN TO WAIT FOR MACBETH AND SEE HE IS DEEP IN THOUGHT. BANQUO KNOWS WHY, AND TRIES TO MAKE LIGHT OF IT.

BANQUO

See how lost our partner is in his thoughts.

BANQUO

Look, how our partner's rapt.

Note: Banquo says "our partner" rather than using Macbeth's name. Banquo fears the glory is all going to Macbeth, he feels he earned an equal share.

MACBETH

(*still in thought*) Well, if fate will have me as king, then let fate crown me without my intervention.

MACBETH

(*aside*) If chance will have me king, why, chance may crown me
Without my stir.

BANQUO AND THE OTHERS ARE STILL WAITING FOR MACBETH.

Act I Scene III. A Deserted Heath.

BANQUO

(*to Ross and Angus*) New honours overwhelm him, like new clothes they'll take a while for him to be comfortable with.

MACBETH

(*in thought*) Even so, time still goes on come what may,

There's an end to even the roughest day.

BANQUO

New honors come upon him,

Like our strange garments, cleave not to their mould

But with the aid of use.

MACBETH

(*aside*) Come what come may,

Time and the hour runs through the roughest day.

> Note: Because "the hour" is inserted here, it could also mean there will be a favourable window of opportunity to do a horrible deed. Like the one he had just decided he wouldn't do – kill the king. He is wavering.
>
> Macbeth finishes his soliloquy with a rhyming couplet.

BANQUO

Noble Macbeth, we await your company.

BANQUO

Worthy Macbeth, we stay upon your leisure.

BANQUO'S WORDS WAKEN MACBETH FROM HIS DAYDREAMING.

SHAKING HIS HEAD HE STEERS HIS MOUNT TO JOIN THE OTHERS.

MACBETH

Forgive me. My mind was elsewhere, I was forgetting myself. But rest assured, kind gentlemen, your efforts are noted on a fresh page in my memory where I cannot forget them. Let us ride to the King.

MACBETH

Give me your favor; my dull brain was wrought With things forgotten. Kind gentlemen, your pains

Are register'd where every day I turn

The leaf to read them. Let us toward the king.

MACBETH TURNS TO SPEAK TO BANQUO IN CONFIDENCE.

MACBETH (CON'T)

(*to Banquo only*) Think about our chance meeting earlier, Banquo. When we've had time to weigh up the implications, we need to share our thoughts on the matter.

BANQUO

Gladly.

MACBETH

Until then – keep it to yourself.

(*shouted to all*) Come, friends.

MACBETH

Think upon what hath chanced, and at more time,

The interim having weigh'd it, let us speak Our free hearts each to other.

BANQUO

Very gladly.

MACBETH

Till then, enough. Come, friends.

MACBETH GALLOPS AHEAD, THE OTHERS FOLLOW BEHIND.

35

ACT I SCENE IV

THE KING'S PALACE AT FORRES.

KING DUNCAN IS HOLDING COURT WITH HIS LORDS IN THE GREAT HALL.
HE IS A LIKABLE RULER. THE KING IS IN JUBILANT MOOD.

MALCOLM, ELDEST SON OF KING DUNCAN, ENTERS THE HALL.

KING DUNCAN Ah, Malcolm! Has Cawdor been executed? Have the officers overseeing it returned yet?	DUNCAN Is execution done on Cawdor? Are not Those in commission yet return'd?
PRINCE MALCOLM They are not yet back, father, but I have spoken with one who witnessed his death. He reported that Cawdor openly confessed his treason, before begging the pardon of your highness and announcing his deep repentance. He was more honourable leaving his life than he was in living it. He died as if he'd rehearsed his death scene, throwing away the dearest thing he owned as if it were a mere trifle.	MALCOLM My liege, They are not yet come back. But I have spoke With one that saw him die, who did report That very frankly he confess'd his treasons, Implored your highness' pardon, and set forth A deep repentance. Nothing in his life Became him like the leaving it; he died As one that had been studied in his death, To throw away the dearest thing he owed As 'twere a careless trifle.

Note: This is another veiled reference to the Gunpowder Plot which is explored later in the 'Porter Scene' (Act 2, Scene 3). Guy Fawkes was caught red-handed in a Catholic plot to blow up Parliament and the king. He was tortured and sentenced to a very cruel public death. Rather than endure a slow public death he jumped off the scaffold, killing himself, 'throwing away the dearest thing...'

KING DUNCAN There's no telling the make up of a man's mind from his appearance. He was once a gentleman in whom I had absolute trust...	DUNCAN There's no art To find the mind's construction in the face: He was a gentleman on whom I built An absolute trust...

ROSS, ANGUS, MACBETH, AND BANQUO ENTER THE HALL INTERRUPTING
THE KING WHO JOYOUSLY HOLDS OUT HIS OPEN ARMS AND STEPS
TOWARDS MACBETH, EMBRACING HIM IN AN UN-KINGLY MANNER.

Note: Note the timing of Macbeth's arrival. The King is lamenting the betrayal of a man he trusted, then greets Macbeth lovingly – who is a much bigger threat.

Act I Scene IV. The King's Palace at Forres.

KING DUNCAN (CONT'D)

(*Joyful*) My praiseworthy cousin! Macbeth, the guilt of my ingratitude lies heavily on me. You have achieved so much that even my swiftest recompense would struggle to catch up with the debt I owe you.

DUNCAN

O worthiest cousin!
The sin of my ingratitude even now
Was heavy on me. Thou art so far before,
That swiftest wing of recompense is slow
To overtake thee.

THE KING BREAKS THE EMBRACE. BANQUO STUDIES
MACBETH'S BEHAVIOUR. MACBETH HAS CHANGED.
THE SEEDS OF MISTRUST ARE FORMING IN BANQUO'S MIND.

KING DUNCAN (CONT'D)

Had you deserved less, the balance of thanks and payment might have been in my favour.
And now, all that is left for me to say;
More are you due than any man can pay!

DUNCAN

Would thou hadst less deserved,
That the proportion both of thanks and payment
Might have been mine! Only I have left to say,
More is thy due than more than all can pay.

MACBETH BOWS TO THE KING.

MACBETH

Serving my king and country is reward enough in itself, my lord. In accepting our service to the throne and its heirs and servants, your highness pays us in full. We merely perform our duty in keeping your good self and your honour safe.

MACBETH

The service and the loyalty I owe,
In doing it, pays itself. Your highness' part
Is to receive our duties, and our duties
Are to your throne and state, children and
  servants,
Which do but what they should, by doing every
  thing
Safe toward your love and honor.

KING DUNCAN

You are welcome here. I have begun to plant the seeds for your future, and will labour to see them bloom and grow.

DUNCAN

Welcome hither.
I have begun to plant thee, and will labor
To make thee full of growing.

THE KING TURNS TOWARDS BANQUO WITH OPEN ARMS.

KING DUNCAN (CONT'D)

Noble Banquo, you are no less deserving, and shall be equally rewarded for your efforts. Let me embrace you, and hold you to my heart.

DUNCAN

Noble Banquo,
That hast no less deserved, nor must be known
No less to have done so; let me enfold thee
And hold thee to my heart.

THE KING EMBRACES BANQUO. ALTHOUGH HE SAYS HE IS AS DESERVING,
THE PRAISE FOR MACBETH WAS GREATER. BANQUO IS A LITTLE PUT OUT.

BANQUO

(*being embraced*) Where, should I bloom and grow, the harvest shall be yours to reap.

BANQUO

There if I grow,
The harvest is your own.

THE KING BREAKS THE EMBRACE AND TURNS BANQUO AROUND.

IT IS NOW MACBETH'S TURN TO NOTICE A CHANGE IN BEHAVIOUR,
THIS TIME OF HIS CLOSE PARTNER IN BATTLE, BANQUO.

THE KING HAS A TEAR IN HIS EYE.

KING DUNCAN

My joy overwhelms me. It seeks to hide behind teardrops meant for sorrow.

DUNCAN

My plenteous joys,
Wanton in fullness, seek to hide themselves
In drops of sorrow.

THE KING PLACES HIS HAND ON MACBETH'S SHOULDER,
TURNING HIM TOWARDS ALL THOSE GATHERED.

KING DUNCAN (CONT'D)

Sons, relatives, lords, and those dear to me, I want it known that we will establish our Kingdom by naming my successor...

DUNCAN

Sons, kinsmen, thanes,
And you whose places are the nearest, know
We will establish our estate upon...

THE KING PAUSES, HIS HAND STILL ON MACBETH'S SHOULDER.

MACBETH IS EXPECTING TO BE NAMED, ESPECIALLY
AFTER SO MUCH PRAISE AND THE WITCHES' PROMISE.

KING DUNCAN (CONT'D)

...my eldest son, Malcolm, who shall henceforth be known as the Prince of Cumberland...

DUNCAN

Our eldest, Malcolm, whom we name hereafter
The Prince of Cumberland,

THE KING PLACES HIS HAND UPON THE SHOULDER OF HIS ELDEST SON,
MALCOLM. EVERYONE LOOKS SURPRISED FOR A MOMENT, NONE MORE SO
THAN MACBETH. THEIR SURPRISE QUICKLY TURNING TO FAWNING
SOUNDS OF AGREEMENT AND APPROVAL.

KING DUNCAN (CONT'D)

(*over the noise of approval*) This is only one honour of the many I shall bestow. Medals of valour will shine like stars on all deservers.

DUNCAN

which honor must
Not unaccompanied invest him only,
But signs of nobleness, like stars, shall shine
On all deservers.

EVERYONE VOICES THEIR SUPPORT AND HAPPINESS.

KING DUNCAN (CONT'D)
And now to Inverness, to Macbeth's castle, to further bind our friendship.

DUNCAN
From hence to Inverness,
And bind us further to you.

MACBETH IS TAKEN BY SURPRISE AGAIN, THIS TIME BY THE KING'S SELF INVITATION. THE KING PUTS HIS ARM AROUND MACBETH'S SHOULDER, PATTING IT IN AN ACT OF TRUE FRIENDSHIP AND ADMIRATION. THEY START WALKING TOGETHER AMID MUCH JOLLITY FROM ALL.

MACBETH THINKING WILDLY, REALISES THE KING WILL BE VULNERABLE AT HIS HOME. HE TURNS AND MAKES A SUGGESTION.

MACBETH
Do not concern yourself with arrangements. I myself will ride ahead and deliver the joyful news of your imminent arrival to my wife.
(*he bows*) So, humbly, I take my leave.

MACBETH
The rest is labor which is not used for you:
I'll be myself the harbinger, and make joyful
The hearing of my wife with your approach;
So humbly take my leave.

Note: 'Harbinger' - a person sent ahead to arrange lodgings for a noble person.

KING DUNCAN
My noble Lord of Cawdor!

DUNCAN
My worthy Cawdor!

THE KING BOWS BACK. MACBETH WALKS AWAY DEEP IN THOUGHT.

MACBETH
(*to self, leaving*) The Prince of Cumberland! An unexpected hurdle to trip me up. One I must leap over if I am to succeed in my aim.
For in my way it lies. Stars douse your fires;
Let darkness hide my black and deep
*   desires:*
Let eyes be blind to my hand's deadly deed,
Yet what they fear to see, let it succeed.

MACBETH
(*aside*)
The Prince of Cumberland! That is a step
On which I must fall down, or else o'erleap,
For in my way it lies. Stars, hide your fires;
Let not light see my black and deep desires:
The eye wink at the hand; yet let that be
Which the eye fears, when it is done, to see.

Note: In Scotland, the King was not automatically succeeded by his eldest son until the rule of David some 80 years after Macbeth lived. Macbeth (a first cousin to the King) would have been rightly expecting himself to be named after the Witches' prophesy and the King's praise. Now an extra hurdle has been thrown in his path to succeed the throne.

Spoiler alert This fact seems to be overlooked. When Macbeth kills the King later on but does not kill his sons even though he has easy opportunity to do so. When the eldest son flees, not staying to take up his rightful title, it makes it conveniently easy for Macbeth to become King. Did Shakespeare have a reason for this? Apparently so. In Holinshed's history, it states that Duncan handed the title to his son, but if he was not of an age able to succeed the rule it would instead be handed to the next in line... Macbeth. Macbeth had to act quickly.

AS MACBETH LEAVES, THE KING TURNS TO BANQUO.

KING DUNCAN	DUNCAN
My true and noble, Banquo! Macbeth is so valiant, the praise he receives feeds my soul;	True, worthy Banquo! He is full so valiant, And in his commendations I am fed;
It is a banquet to me, let's follow him.	*It is a banquet to me. Let's after him,*
He heeds not his welfare to bid us welcome:	*Whose care is gone before to bid us welcome:*
A true kinsman above all other men.	It is a peerless kinsman.

BANQUO WATCHES THE DEPARTING MACBETH WITH NAGGING DOUBT FORMING IN HIS MIND.

FANFARE SOUNDS AS THE KING EXITS WITH THE LORDS.

> *Historical: Cumberland is a county in the northwest of England, it switched back and forth between Scottish and English rule through the centuries. 'Prince of Cumberland' was a title given to the heir to the Scottish throne.*
>
> *Inverness is a town in Scotland about twenty-five miles from the king's palace at Forres, however, Glamis Castle which Macbeth inherited from his father, is the opposite end of Scotland in Angus, near Dundee. Cawdor Castle is indeed near Inverness, but it was not built until the 14th Century, long after Macbeth died. Some confusion of facts in the play.*
>
> *Malcolm II was murdered at the town of Cawdor, a violent death, referred to in chronicles as a 'kingslaying'. His grandson, a young Duncan I became king thereafter. He was killed when he attacked Macbeth's army at Elgin in Moray six years later and Macbeth was subsequently crowned king at Scone.*

> *Holinshed's inaccurate historical work, which was Shakespeare's source, had witches, prophesy, treason, execution and murder, all topics that were an obsession of King James. Shakespeare wrote the play for a special royal performance at Hampton Court performed in 1606 before King James and his brother-in-law, Christian IV, King of Denmark. Shakespeare also made the Vikings Norwegian so as not to upset the Danish King and his sister, James' wife.*
>
> *Shakespeare's Macbeth is best considered a fantasy based very loosely on fact. Shakespeare's modus operandi was to take a history or an existing story and rework it as his own, something he was exceptionally good at. It allowed him greater scope to concentrate on the characters, the story was already there.*
>
> *Trivia: King James married his Danish wife, Anne, then aged fifteen, at Kronborg Castle in Elsinore. If that sounds familiar, it is the castle Hamlet's Elsinore Castle was based on.*

ACT I SCENE V

MACBETH'S CASTLE. THE DRAWING ROOM.

LADY MACBETH IS ALONE IN THE CASTLE DRAWING ROOM.

A SERVANT HANDS HER A LETTER. RECOGNISING THE SEAL, SHE EXCITEDLY
TEARS IT OPEN, SCANNING THE LETTER RAPIDLY.

> Note: Lady Macbeth speaks in prose while reading the letter rather than the
> usual blank verse (poetry that doesn't rhyme).

LADY MACBETH

(*reading letter*) "I met them on the day of our victory, and have since learnt by the accuracy of their report that they have more than mere mortal knowledge. When I pressured them further they vanished into thin air. While I stood in disbelief and wonder, officers of the King arrived, announcing me as *'New Lord of Cawdor.'* The same title the weird women had greeted me with before referring to a further title with, *'Praise, King that shall be!'*

LADY MACBETH

"They met me in the day of success, and I have learned by the perfectest report, they have more in them than mortal knowledge. When I burned in desire to question them further, they made themselves air, into which they vanished. Whiles I stood rapt in the wonder of it, came missives from the King, who all-hailed me 'Thane of Cawdor'; by which title, before, these weird sisters saluted me, and referred me to the coming on of time with 'Hail, King that shalt be!'

SHE PAUSES, STUNNED BY THIS THOUGHT,
THEN CARRIES ON READING EXCITEDLY.

LADY MACBETH (CONT'D)

"I thought it wise to deliver this news to you, my dearest partner in greatness, so you may lose no time in celebrating the greatness which is promised you. Keep it close to your heart, and farewell."

LADY MACBETH

"This have I thought good to deliver thee, my dearest partner of greatness, that thou mightst not lose the dues of rejoicing, by being ignorant of what greatness is promised thee. Lay it to thy heart, and farewell."

SHE STOPS READING THE LETTER, HOLDING IT TO HER CHEST
AND VOICING HER THOUGHTS.

LADY MACBETH (CONT'D)	LADY MACBETH
(*aside, in thought*) Glamis you are, and now Cawdor too, and you shall be what you are promised. But I fear you are too full of the milk of human kindness to take the swiftest route. You want greatness - you are not without ambition - but you lack the ruthlessness to go with it. You'd seek to earn it by noble means, yet by foul means you could take it.	Glamis thou art, and Cawdor, and shalt be What thou art promised. Yet do I fear thy nature; It is too full o' the milk of human kindness To catch the nearest way. Thou wouldst be great; Art not without ambition, but without The illness should attend it. What thou wouldst highly, That wouldst thou holily; wouldst not play false, And yet wouldst wrongly win.

LADY MACBETH FOLDS THE LETTER, GOES TO HER WRITING DESK
AND RESEALS IT WITH WAX. SHE WRITES SOMETHING ON IT.

SHE TAKES A KEY FROM A SILVER CASE IN THE DESK, UNLOCKS A
DRAWER, THEN PUTS THE LETTER IN IT, RELOCKING IT.

LADY MACBETH (CONT'D)	LADY MACBETH
(*speaking her thoughts*) Great Glamis, that which you desire calls for '*that*' which you must do. Yet, '*that*' you are afraid to do, no matter how highly you desire it. Hurry home, so I may pour my spirit into your ear, and with the strength of my tongue, chase away all that impedes you from obtaining the 'golden circle', which fate and spiritual aid seem to have crowned you with.	Thou'ldst have, great Glamis, That which cries, "Thus thou must do," if thou have it; And that which rather thou dost fear to do Than wishest should be undone. Hie thee hither, That I may pour my spirits in thine ear, And chastise with the valor of my tongue All that impedes thee from the golden round, Which fate and metaphysical aid doth seem To have thee crown'd withal.

Note: 'Golden round' is the royal crown.

THE SERVANT RE-ENTERS IN HASTE.

LADY MACBETH (CONT'D)	LADY MACBETH
(*concerned*) What is your message?	What is your tidings?
SERVANT	MESSENGER
(*urgent*) The King is coming here tonight.	The King comes here tonight.
LADY MACBETH	LADY MACBETH
You are mad to say such a thing! Isn't your master with him? If it were true we would have been informed us so we could make preparations.	Thou'rt mad to say it! Is not thy master with him? who, were't so, Would have inform'd for preparation.

42

SERVANT	MESSENGER
My lady, if you please, it is true. Our Lord is coming too. A messenger ran ahead of him, almost dead from exhaustion he had scarcely enough breath to deliver this message.	So please you, it is true: our Thane is coming. One of my fellows had the speed of him, Who, almost dead for breath, had scarcely more Than would make up his message.
LADY MACBETH	LADY MACBETH
Then tend to him well, he brings great news.	Give him tending; He brings great news.

AS THE MESSENGER LEAVES A RAVEN CRIES OUT FROM THE RAFTERS, (THE MESSENGER OF DEATH). LADY MACBETH STARTS AT THE SOUND.

LADY MACBETH (CONT'D)	LADY MACBETH
(aside, looking up at the raven) The raven, the messenger of death itself, is hoarse announcing the fateful arrival of King Duncan within my battlements.	The raven himself is hoarse That croaks the fatal entrance of Duncan Under my battlements.

SHE HEARS WINGS FLUTTERING AWAY AND PAUSES.

Note: Link to witches - the raven was thought to be the harbinger of death. Witches were believed to be able to change form into a raven and spy or fly away evading capture. The raven sounds hoarse like the messenger.

LADY MACBETH (CONT'D)	LADY MACBETH
Come, spirits who govern mortal thoughts, purge my female weakness and fill me from top to toe with your cruel, evil ways! Thicken my blood, quash my remorse, lest my conscience shake me from my purpose and come between me and the deed. Come to my womanly breasts all you murdering spirits of mischief and disaster, and replace my milk with gall. And come, dark night, wrap yourself in the thickest, foulest smoke from hell, to keep my keen knife from seeing the wound it inflicts and heaven from peeping through the blanket of darkness to cry, "Stop! Stop!"	Come, you spirits That tend on mortal thoughts, unsex me here And fill me, from the crown to the toe, top-full Of direst cruelty! Make thick my blood, Stop up the access and passage to remorse, That no compunctious visitings of nature Shake my fell purpose nor keep peace between The effect and it! Come to my woman's breasts, And take my milk for gall, you murdering ministers, Wherever in your sightless substances You wait on nature's mischief! Come, thick night, And pall thee in the dunnest smoke of hell, That my keen knife see not the wound it makes, Nor heaven peep through the blanket of the dark To cry, "Hold, hold!"

SHE OPENS A DESK COMPARTMENT, LOOKS AT A BEJEWELLED DAGGER
STORED INSIDE IT FOR A MOMENT, THEN CLOSES IT AGAIN. SHE RUSHES
FROM THE ROOM, TIDYING THINGS ON THE WAY. THERE IS A LOT TO DO
IN A SHORT TIME IF THE KING IS ARRIVING.

MACBETH'S CASTLE. LATER THAT DAY.

MACBETH'S CASTLE IS IN TURMOIL, MAKING READY FOR THE KING'S VISIT.

LADY MACBETH IS BUSY ORDERING STAFF ABOUT IN THE CASTLE.

FOOD IS PREPARED, ORNAMENTS POLISHED, FIRES LIT, FLOORS SCRUBBED,
FRESH FLOWERS AND SCENTED GARLANDS DISTRIBUTED, WINE AND BEER
KEGS ROLLED INTO POSITION, FRESHLY KILLED HOGS TIED AND CARRIED IN
ON POLES BY SERVANTS, POTS BOILING, STAFF SCURRYING.

OUTSIDE THE CASTLE, MACBETH ARRIVES HARD AND FAST. HE LEAPS FROM
HIS HORSE AND BURSTS IN, TIRED AND DIRTY FROM THE JOURNEY.

LADY MACBETH RUSHES TO HIM, EMBRACING HIM, KISSING HIS FACE
FURIOUSLY, OBLIVIOUS TO THE STATE OF HIM. HE PICKS HER UP AND
CARRIES HER TO THEIR ROOM. SHE STILL KISSES HIM WILDLY. THE POWER
HAS MADE HER LUST FOR HIM.

LADY MACBETH (*excited while kissing him repeatedly*) Great Glamis! Worthy Cawdor! Even greater to follow according to the prophecy! Your letter has transported me beyond the present, I feel the future is here and now.	LADY MACBETH Great Glamis! Worthy Cawdor! Greater than both, by the all-hail hereafter! Thy letters have transported me beyond This ignorant present, and I feel now The future in the instant.
MACBETH My dearest love...	MACBETH My dearest love,

HE HOLDS HER AWAY, LOOKING INTO HER EYES.

MACBETH (CONT'D) King Duncan comes here tonight.	MACBETH Duncan comes here tonight.

SHE WALKS HER FINGERS SEDUCTIVELY UP HIS CHEST -
AS IF THERE IS A SECRET TO HIDE.

LADY MACBETH (*suggesting he may never leave*) But '*when*' does he leave?	LADY MACBETH And when goes hence?

Act I Scene V. Macbeth's Castle.

SHE STOPS HER FINGERS, LOOKING HARD INTO MACBETH'S EYES.

MACBETH

He 'plans' to leave tomorrow.

LADY MACBETH

Oh, he'll not see tomorrow's light!

MACBETH

Tomorrow, as he purposes.

LADY MACBETH

O, never
Shall sun that morrow see!

SHE MAKES HER FINGERS FALL AS IF A MAN FALLING DOWN DEAD.

SHE STUDIES MACBETH'S FACE WHICH REFLECTS HIS DARK THOUGHTS.

SHE LOOKS AT HIM WORRIEDLY.

LADY MACBETH (CONT'D)

Your face, my lord, is like an open book
where men may read between the lines.
To deceive the onlooker, you must look
the way the onlooker expects; a
welcome in your eye, in your hand, and
in your tongue. Look the innocent
flower, be the serpent hiding beneath.
Our guest must be entertained, leave the
'greater' business to me.
That which for all of our days shall bring,
The ultimate power of the sovereign.

LADY MACBETH

Your face, my Thane, is as a book where men
May read strange matters. To beguile the time,
Look like the time; bear welcome in your eye,
Your hand, your tongue; look like the innocent
  flower,
But be the serpent under't. He that's coming
Must be provided for; and you shall put
This night's great business into my dispatch,
Which shall to all our nights and days to come
Give solely sovereign sway and masterdom.

> Note: A reference to the Gunpowder Plot. To commemorate discovering and
> preventing the plot to assassinate him, King James had a medal created
> picturing a snake hiding amongst flowers. A reference to the medal is made
> when Lady Macbeth tells her husband to "look like the innocent flower, but be
> the serpent under it". See Act II, Scene III for more detail.

MACBETH

We'll speak later.

MACBETH

We will speak further.

MACBETH FREEZES AT THE WINDOW, SEEING THE KING APPROACH WITH
HIS ENTOURAGE. HIS MIND IS SEIZED WITH THE ENORMITY OF WHAT IS TO
COME. LADY MACBETH IS GRIPPED IN COLD TERROR BY HIS EXPRESSION.

LADY MACBETH

Try to look normal inside,
An altered appearance shows something to
  hide.
Leave the rest to me.

LADY MACBETH

Only look up clear;
To alter favor ever is to fear:
Leave all the rest to me.

Note: She says she'll do the 'great business', 'leave all the rest to me'. but later she finds she cannot as the King reminds her of her father. Macbeth has to do it.

Important Note: *In the play there does not seem to have been time for Macbeth to have written the letter and had it delivered, as he rode straight to the King and from there straight to his home. We must allow for artistic licence here, and not over-analyse every small detail, no artistic work would stand up to centuries of analysis without some flaws being spotted. However, this gives further weight to the theory that the play is from a heavily edited source, such as a prompt book. The events which are skipped may well have once been present and would fill in the missing time and details, but sadly there is no surviving copy of a longer text.*

ACT I SCENE VI

OUTSIDE MACBETH'S CASTLE.

THE KING ARRIVES AT MACBETH'S CASTLE THAT EVENING. HE IS ACCOMPANIED BY HIS SONS, MALCOLM AND DONALBAIN, AND THE LORDS, BANQUO, LENNOX, MACDUFF, ROSS, AND ANGUS, ALONG WITH VARIOUS ROYAL ATTENDANTS.

THEY PULL UP OUTSIDE THE CASTLE.

KING DUNCAN

This castle is pleasantly situated. The air freshly scented and most agreeable to the senses.

BANQUO

Indeed, your highness. Look, the house martin makes himself guest this summer, proof the smell of heaven's breath is most seductive here. There's not a buttress, eave or favourable cove this bird has not made a nest for its young. I've noticed the air is most pleasant where they choose to live and breed.

DUNCAN

This castle hath a pleasant seat; the air
Nimbly and sweetly recommends itself
Unto our gentle senses.

BANQUO

This guest of summer,
The temple-haunting martlet, does approve
By his loved mansionry that the heaven's breath
Smells wooingly here. No jutty, frieze,
Buttress, nor coign of vantage, but this bird
Hath made his pendant bed and procreant cradle;
Where they most breed and haunt, I have observed
The air is delicate.

LADY MACBETH RUSHES OUT TO GREET THEM, CURTSEYING.

Note: The line beginning, "By his loved mansionry...", has one extra syllable, and the following line, "Smells wooingly here...", is one syllable short. However, by combining the two lines, the word count is correct.

The house martin (martlet) is a small black and white songbird of the swallow family, often building its nest on the walls of buildings.

'Jutty' - protruding brick work. 'Frieze' - a decorative strip between the roof and the building. 'Coign' - corner or cove formed at the angle of a roof.

KING DUNCAN

Look, see! Our honoured hostess! The love we are shown is often a burden which we endure out of love. May my example teach you to show love for us who burden you and may God reward you for your pains.

DUNCAN

See, see, our honor'd hostess!
The love that follows us sometime is our trouble,
Which still we thank as love. Herein I teach you
How you shall bid God 'ild us for your pains,
And thank us for your trouble.

LADY MACBETH

Our service to yourself, even if doubled, then doubled again is nothing compared to the immense honour your Majesty bestows upon our family. For past honours and these present ones heaped on top, we remain your humble servants.

LADY MACBETH

All our service
In every point twice done, and then done double,
Were poor and single business to contend
Against those honors deep and broad wherewith
Your Majesty loads our house. For those of old,
And the late dignities heap'd up to them,
We rest your hermits.

> Note: "We rest your hermits" makes little sense in translation. Hermits followed the King and prayed for him. Their number was equal to the age of the king, so every birthday one more was added. Lady Macbeth is saying that she and her husband will pray so hard that the king's hermits can rest a while.

KING DUNCAN

Where's the new Lord of Cawdor? I chased him down, hoping to be here to welcome him. But he rides well, and his great love for you has spurred him to his home before me.

DUNCAN

Where's the Thane of Cawdor?
We coursed him at the heels and had a purpose
To be his purveyor; but he rides well,
And his great love, sharp as his spur, hath holp him
To his home before us.

> Note: The King uses the 'royal we'. When he says 'we' or 'us' he means himself. He is the ruler, he represents (and owns) everyone. The plural has been replaced by the singular in the translation (e.g. 'we' becomes 'I') as it makes little sense to anyone who is not familiar with the language of royals.

THE KING DISMOUNTS FOLLOWED BY HIS ENTOURAGE.

HE TAKES HER HAND, AND KISSES IT, LOOKING INTO HER EYES
WITH A ROGUISH SMILE.

KING DUNCAN (CONT'D)

Beautiful and noble hostess, I am 'your' guest tonight.

DUNCAN

Fair and noble hostess,
We are your guest tonight.

HE DROPS HER HAND AND BOWS TO HER.
LADY MACBETH CURTSEYS AGAIN IN RESPONSE.

LADY MACBETH

We remain your servants as ever, and our servants, and all we possess, are rightfully yours, and ever available at your majesty's pleasure, to claim as his own.

LADY MACBETH

Your servants ever
Have theirs, themselves, and what is theirs, in
   compt,
To make their audit at your Highness' pleasure,
Still to return your own.

SHE SMILES AT THE KING WITH A TWINKLE IN HER EYES.

Note: By law, the King owned all the Macbeth's property, including their lives. She is fawningly acknowledging this, with the added tease of offering more than property to flatter the King, and to make him feel safe and relaxed, thereby making the planned deed easier.

KING DUNCAN

Give me your hand. Lead me to my host. I regard him highly and shall continue my pleasantries with him. (*Offering his arm*) With your permission, my hostess.

DUNCAN

Give me your hand;
Conduct me to mine host. We love him highly,
And shall continue our graces towards him.
By your leave, hostess.

SHE TAKES HIS ARM AND LEADS HIM INTO THE CASTLE.

ACT I SCENE VII

Macbeth's Castle. Outside the Great Hall.

STAFF BUSTLE TO AND FRO SERVING A GIANT FEAST IN THE GREAT HALL.
SOUNDS OF MERRIMENT ECHO FROM WITHIN THE HALL.

MACBETH SITS ALONE OUTSIDE THE HALL, FRAUGHT IN HIS THOUGHTS.

> Note: Original version included a 'sewer' serving, he is chief butler.
>
> This is Macbeth's second soliloquy. It is important as this is his last rational speech where he is still able to decide against doing the deed or carrying it out and being forever damned.

MACBETH	MACBETH
(*struggling with his thoughts*) If, when done it's done and over, then the quicker it's done the better. If the assassination could sweep away all consequence, leaving only success in the wake of his demise, and if this act was the be-all and end-all of it here, right here, this side of eternity, we'd chance the afterlife to come. But there is still divine judgement to contend with here in this life: if we teach bloody deeds, the bloody deeds return to plague the teacher. The natural justice which guides the ingredients of our poisoned cup back to our own lips.	If it were done when 'tis done, then 'twere well It were done quickly. If the assassination Could trammel up the consequence, and catch, With his surcease, success; that but this blow Might be the be-all and the end-all here, But here, upon this bank and shoal of time, We'd jump the life to come. But in these cases We still have judgement here, that we but teach Bloody instructions, which being taught return To plague the inventor. This even-handed justice Commends the ingredients of our poison'd chalice

A LOUD RAUCOUS ROAR ERUPTS FROM THE NEXT ROOM.

MACBETH (CONT'D)	MACBETH
(*talking himself out of it*) By staying here, he puts his trust in me for two reasons: First, I'm related to him and a loyal subject; strong arguments against the deed. Second, as his host, I'm expected to shut the door against any murderer – not carry the knife myself.	To our own lips. He's here in double trust: First, as I am his kinsman and his subject, Strong both against the deed; then, as his host, Who should against his murderer shut the door, Not bear the knife myself.

MORE STAFF BUSTLE BY CARRYING ITEMS.

MACBETH (CONT'D)

Besides, the King has not abused his powers; so faultless has his ruling been that his virtues will plead like angels crying out against the deep damnation of his removal. And pity – like that for a naked new-born babe caught in a storm, or for heaven's messengers tossed on the invisible wings of a hurricane – shall blow news of the dreadful deed like dust in every eye, and the tears will drown the wind.

MACBETH

Besides, this Duncan
Hath borne his faculties so meek, hath been
So clear in his great office, that his virtues
Will plead like angels trumpet-tongued against
The deep damnation of his taking-off,
And pity, like a naked new-born babe,
Striding the blast, or heaven's cherubin horsed
Upon the sightless couriers of the air,
Shall blow the horrid deed in every eye,
That tears shall drown the wind.

> *Note: 'Cherubin' – the word 'cherubin' doesn't exist. A 'cherub' is a high ranking angel. Most editors believe the plural 'cherubim' is correct here. The order of angels are ranked in nine levels: angels, archangels, principalities, powers, virtues, dominions, thrones, cherubim, and seraphim.*
>
> *Macbeth rarely says death, murder etc. He uses vague terms or similes. Here he says, 'removal'.*

INSIDE THE GREAT HALL.

THE KING LEANS OVER TO LADY MACBETH, SAYING SOMETHING IN HER EAR AND GESTURING TO THE EMPTY SEAT MACBETH HAD OCCUPIED.

LADY MACBETH STANDS, CURTSEYS TO THE MERRY KING, LEANS IN AND WITH A SMILE WHISPERS SOMETHING IN HIS EAR.

THE KING LAUGHS AND RAISES HIS GOBLET IN APPROVAL.

LADY MACBETH WALKS FROM THE HALL, DETERMINED.

Outside The Great Hall.

MACBETH (CONT'D)	MACBETH
(*still thinking*) I have nothing to spur me on and urge me forward, except leaping ambition, which in over-reaching itself most often causes its own downfall...	I have no spur To prick the sides of my intent, but only Vaulting ambition, which o'erleaps itself And falls on the other —

> Note: A metaphor on horse riding. Spurs are used to 'prick the sides' of a horse to urge it into action. His vaulting ambition overleaps itself – as in vaulting onto a horse in such a rush that he falls over the other side.

LADY MACBETH BURSTS THROUGH THE LARGE HALL DOORS – INTERRUPTING MACBETH'S THOUGHTS - CONCERNED, ANGRY, AND RIGHT ON CUE TO URGE MACBETH ON.

MACBETH LOOKS UP AT HER ENTRANCE.

MACBETH (CONT'D)	MACBETH
Well wife? What's happening?	How now, what news?
LADY MACBETH	**LADY MACBETH**
He's almost finished dining. Why have you left the room?	He has almost supp'd. Why have you left the chamber?
MACBETH	**MACBETH**
Has he asked after me?	Hath he ask'd for me?
LADY MACBETH	**LADY MACBETH**
What do you think!	Know you not he has?

> Note: Of course he will have asked after him. The King came here to honour Macbeth with his royal presence.

HE SLUMPS BACK DOWN AGAIN, RESIGNED TO HIS PREVIOUS THOUGHTS.

MACBETH	MACBETH
We'll not proceed with this matter.	We will proceed no further in this business:

SHE REACTS WITH HORROR, KNOWING THIS IS THEIR ONE BIG CHANCE.

SHE BUSTLES HIM INTO A MORE PRIVATE ANTECHAMBER CLOSING THE DOOR DETERMINEDLY BEHIND THEM.

MACBETH (CONT'D)

He has just honoured me, and my bravery has brought glowing accounts from all ranks. This should be flaunted like new clothes, not cast aside so soon.

LADY MACBETH

(*scornfully hissed*) Was it drunken ambition you dressed yourself in before? Has it been sleeping since? Has it awoken hung-over to see what it did in a sober light? Now I see what your love for me is worth. Are you afraid to be as brave in your actions as you are in your ambitions? How can you procure the 'golden' reward, which you hold in such high esteem, while behaving like a coward of such low esteem? – Saying, *"I'd like to"*, followed by, *"but I daren't"*, like the proverbial cat who wants the fish, but won't get his feet wet!

MACBETH

He hath honor'd me of late, and I have bought
Golden opinions from all sorts of people,
Which would be worn now in their newest gloss,
Not cast aside so soon.

LADY MACBETH

Was the hope drunk
Wherein you dress'd yourself? Hath it slept since?
And wakes it now, to look so green and pale
At what it did so freely? From this time
Such I account thy love. Art thou afeard
To be the same in thine own act and valor
As thou art in desire? Wouldst thou have that
Which thou esteem'st the ornament of life
And live a coward in thine own esteem,
Letting "I dare not" wait upon "I would"
Like the poor cat i' the adage?

HE REACTS ANGRILY. HER ACCUSATIONS OF COWARDICE HAVE WORKED.

MACBETH

Enough woman! There's nothing I wouldn't dare do. Any man who dares more is not human.

MACBETH

Prithee, peace!
I dare do all that may become a man;
Who dares do more is none.

LADY MACBETH

What creature was it then that shared this idea with me? When you dared do it, then you were a man. By carrying out what you had dared; much more a man. Before, neither time nor place were right, and yet you would have arranged for them both to be so. Now they have arranged themselves, yet, handed such perfect opportunity you daren't do it? I have suckled before, and know how tender is the love for the baby upon my breast. But while it smiled up at me, I would have pulled my nipple from its toothless gums and dashed its brains out had I, like you, sworn to do so.

LADY MACBETH

What beast was't then
That made you break this enterprise to me?
When you durst do it, then you were a man;
And, to be more than what you were, you would
Be so much more the man. Nor time nor place
Did then adhere, and yet you would make both:
They have made themselves, and that their fitness
  now
Does unmake you. I have given suck, and know
How tender 'tis to love the babe that milks me:
I would, while it was smiling in my face,
Have pluck'd my nipple from his boneless gums,
And dash'd the brains out, had I so sworn as you
Have done to this.

> Note: From these words it seems they had been plotting the 'enterprise' for some time before. The letter only mentioned the Witches' prophecy.

> Historical Note: They have no children, yet she has suckled, though in Shakespeare's time women of higher status would employ a nursemaid who would breastfeed the baby. The real Lady Macbeth was married and had a son called Lulach by a previous husband, (who Macbeth probably killed as shortly after his death he married his widow). Macbeth's stepson, Lulach, reigned for only a few months after Macbeth died, before being killed by Malcolm III.

MACBETH	MACBETH
And if we fail?	If we should fail?
LADY MACBETH	**LADY MACBETH**
If we fail, we fail! But wind up your courage taut like a bow string and we'll not fail.	We fail! But screw your courage to the sticking-place, And we'll not fail.

> Note: The "sticking-place" is the notch that holds the string of a crossbow when it is ready to fire.

SHE LOWERS HER TONE, MORE POSITIVE NOW.

LADY MACBETH (CONT'D)	LADY MACBETH
When Duncan is asleep – which after his arduous journey will be sound and inviting – I will ply his two attendants with enough wine and festivity to cloud their memory and lose all reasoning. When they sleep like swine, so drunk they may as well be dead, what can't you and I do to the unguarded Duncan? What can't we blame on his drink sodden guards? They shall bear the guilt of our great cull.	When Duncan is asleep — Whereto the rather shall his day's hard journey Soundly invite him — his two chamberlains Will I with wine and wassail so convince, That memory, the warder of the brain, Shall be a fume and the receipt of reason A limbec only. When in swinish sleep Their drenched natures lie as in a death, What cannot you and I perform upon The unguarded Duncan? What not put upon His spongy officers, who shall bear the guilt Of our great quell?

> Note: A 'limbec' – top part of a still, containing nothing but hot air.

MACBETH	MACBETH
You shall bear male children only! Your fearless spirit could produce nothing but males. And after we've marked the two sleeping guards with blood, using their own daggers of course, won't everyone believe they did it?	Bring forth men-children only, For thy undaunted mettle should compose Nothing but males. Will it not be received, When we have mark'd with blood those sleepy two Of his own chamber, and used their very daggers, That they have done't?

LADY MACBETH EXCITEDLY MOVES CLOSER TO HIM
- NOW THAT SHE HAS WON HIM OVER.

LADY MACBETH

Who would dare presume otherwise, since we shall grieve and condemn his death with such vigour?

MACBETH

I am decided. I shall strain every muscle in my body towards this terrible deed.

LADY MACBETH

Who dares receive it other,
As we shall make our griefs and clamor roar
Upon his death?

MACBETH

I am settled, and bend up
Each corporal agent to this terrible feat.

MACBETH HEADS TO THE DOOR

MACBETH (CONT'D)

Come, as pleasant hosts we'll use our wiles,
To hide what false hearts know behind false smiles.

MACBETH

Away, and mock the time with fairest show:
False face must hide what the false heart doth know.

Note: It becomes more obvious now that it's Lady Macbeth who really holds the crown in such high esteem and she doesn't want to let this chance slip by. She is the driving force behind the quest for ultimate power at any cost.

Again, Shakespeare notifies the end of a scene to the audience with a rhyme.

End of Act I

ACT II

IN WHICH A DIRE DEED IS PERFORMED

DON'T HEAR IT DUNCAN, FOR IT IS THE BELL,
WHICH SUMMONS YOU TO HEAVEN – OR TO HELL

ACT II

ACT II SCENE I

THE CASTLE COURTYARD. NIGHT.

BANQUO IS SEATED AT AN OUTSIDE TABLE WITH HIS SON FLEANCE. A BURNING TORCH PROVIDES THEM WITH LIGHT. UPON THE TABLE RESTS A FLAGON OF WINE NEXT TO A METAL GOBLET FROM WHICH BANQUO DRINKS. HE IS DRUNK, BUT NOT OVERLY SO.

BANQUO SEES LADY MACBETH LEADING THE MERRY KING TO HIS ROOM.

A BLACK VELVET BAG LIES ON THE TABLE AND BANQUO IS TURNING A DIAMOND IN HIS HAND, DEEP IN HIS OWN THOUGHTS. HE RETURNS THE DIAMOND TO THE BAG AND PULLS THE DRAW STRING CLOSED.

FLEANCE, HIS SON, A MID-TEENS YOUTH, SITS IDLY BY, OBVIOUSLY BORED, WHITTLING ON A STICK WITH A POCKET KNIFE.

BANQUO IS HAVING DARK THOUGHTS. A MIXTURE OF JEALOUSY, APPREHENSION AT WHAT LIES AHEAD DUE TO THE PROPHECY, AND DESPONDENCY AT THE IMBALANCE OF REWARDS HANDED OUT BY THE KING TO HIMSELF AND TO MACBETH.

HIS MIND WANDERS, HE PICTURES THE PROPHECY AND HE LOOKS AT HIS SON. HE PICTURES THE KING GIVING HIM THE DIAMOND FOR LADY MACBETH. HE PICTURES SEEING THE KING WITH LADY MACBETH. HE IS JEALOUS. HIS MIND THEN ALTERNATES BETWEEN KILLING THE KING HIMSELF IN BATTLE WITH HIS SWORD, AND THEN VISUALISING A JEALOUS SPAT WHERE HE KILLS MACBETH WITH HIS DAGGER.

HE STABS HIS DAGGER INTO THE WOODEN TABLE.

BANQUO	BANQUO
What time is it, boy?	How goes the night, boy?

FLEANCE LOOKS UP AT THE SKY.

FLEANCE	FLEANCE
The moon's gone down, but I've not heard the clock strike.	The moon is down; I have not heard the clock.
BANQUO	BANQUO
It goes down at midnight.	And she goes down at twelve.
FLEANCE	FLEANCE
I'm sure it's later than that, father.	I take't 'tis later, sir.

58

Act II Scene I. Castle Courtyard. Night.

BANQUO LOOKS AT HIS SON AND IMAGINES HIM WITH A CROWN
UPON HIS HEAD AND THE KING LYING ON THE GROUND WITH
BANQUO WITHDRAWING HIS SWORD FROM HIS LIFELESS BODY.
HE WORRIES WHAT HE MAY DO.

BANQUO	BANQUO
Here, take my sword.	Hold, take my sword.

HE PASSES HIS SWORD TO FLEANCE.

HE LOOKS UP AT THE SKY, IT IS OVERCAST, NO STARS VISIBLE.

BANQUO (CONT'D)	BANQUO
There must be a strike in heaven, the candles in the sky are not lit.	There's husbandry in heaven, Their candles are all out.

Note: 'Husbandry' means frugality, saving costs.

HE SEES HIS DAGGER IN THE WOODEN TABLE.

BANQUO (CONT'D)	BANQUO
Take my dagger too. (he yawns) My eyes are like lead and summon me to bed, but I cannot sleep. (he shudders) Merciful God, keep me from the evil thoughts that come with my sleep!	Take thee that too. A heavy summons lies like lead upon me, And yet I would not sleep. Merciful powers, Restrain in me the cursed thoughts that nature Gives way to in repose!

A NOISE IS HEARD. BANQUO IS STILL JUMPY FROM HIS THOUGHTS.

BANQUO (CONT'D)	BANQUO
(to son) Give me my sword.	Give me my sword.

BANQUO TAKES BACK HIS SWORD. HE CAN'T SEE WHERE
THE NOISE IS COMING FROM IN THE DARKNESS.

BANQUO (CONT'D)	BANQUO
Who's there?	Who's there?

A VOICE COMES FROM THE SHADOWS.

MACBETH	MACBETH
(within) A friend, Banquo.	A friend.

MACBETH AND HIS ATTENDANT SETON CASUALLY STEP OUT FROM THE
SHADOWS, AS IF THEY HAD BEEN STANDING THERE LISTENING.

BANQUO

(*relieved*) Macbeth! What, not at rest, sir? The King's in bed. He's been in unusually high spirits, sending large gratuities to your servants. He wanted to thank your wife with this diamond for being such an accommodating hostess. He ended the evening happily contented.

BANQUO

What, sir, not yet at rest? The King's a-bed. He hath been in unusual pleasure and Sent forth great largess to your offices: This diamond he greets your wife withal, By the name of most kind hostess, and shut up In measureless content.

BANQUO THROWS THE BAG TO MACBETH, WHO CATCHES IT, BARELY REACTING. HIS MIND IS ELSEWHERE.

MACBETH

We were taken by surprise, but did our best to serve under the circumstances.

MACBETH

Being unprepared, Our will became the servant to defect, Which else should free have wrought.

BANQUO

It went well.
(*changing subject*) Last night, I dreamt of the three weird women... In your case, so far they've been accurate.

BANQUO

All's well.
I dreamt last night of the three weird sisters: To you they have show'd some truth.

MACBETH

(*lying*) I'd not given them much thought... However when we have an hour to spare we should discuss that business further, if you would grant me the time.

MACBETH

I think not of them: Yet, when we can entreat an hour to serve, We would spend it in some words upon that business, If you would grant the time.

BANQUO

At your convenience.

BANQUO

At your kind'st leisure.

MACBETH

If you should side with me, when the time comes, it will be greatly in your favour.

MACBETH

If you shall cleave to my consent, when 'tis, It shall make honor for you.

BANQUO

(*suspicious*) Providing I lose no favour in doing so, and keep a clear conscience with my allegiance to the King intact, I'd be happy to discuss it.

BANQUO

So I lose none In seeking to augment it, but still keep My bosom franchised and allegiance clear, I shall be counsell'd.

MACBETH

In the meantime, sleep well.

MACBETH

Good repose the while.

BANQUO STANDS TO LEAVE, HE IS APPREHENSIVE OF THIS CONVERSATION, ESPECIALLY AT THIS TIME OF NIGHT, AND MACBETH NEEDS TO GET BANQUO OUT OF THE WAY TO PERFORM THE DEED.

Act II Scene I. Castle Courtyard. Night.

BANQUO	**BANQUO**
Thank you, sir. You too.	Thanks, sir, the like to you.

BANQUO AND FLEANCE LEAVE.

MACBETH PASSES THE JEWEL BAG TO SETON ABSENTMINDEDLY.

MACBETH	**MACBETH**
(*to Seton*) Here. Go tell your mistress to strike the bell when '*my drink is ready'*. Then get yourself to bed.	Go bid thy mistress, when my drink is ready, She strike upon the bell. Get thee to bed.

> *Note: Sounding the bell is Macbeth's cue from his wife that the coast is clear.*

SETON LEAVES WITH THE JEWEL BAG. AS HE HEADS FOR THE STAIRS HE MISSES AND CATCHES A CORNER. HE DRUNKENLY LAUGHS AT HIMSELF.

> *Note: Throughout the play various pages and messengers attend Macbeth, but it makes sense to make his close confident the same man, Seyton, or Seton, depending on which publication you read. Seyton is close to Macbeth's darker side, the fewer assistants who knew that side the better. It may be no coincidence that the word Seyton can be pronounced to sound like 'satan'.*
>
> *A 14th Century verse rhymes the first syllable of Seyton with 'Day'. This rhyme also appears in the volume "Phrophecie", which was published to celebrate the fulfilment of one of Merlin's most celebrated prophecies; the union of Scotland and England.*
>
> *The name derives from a British man named Say who moved to Scotland in the 10th century and adopted the surname Seyton upon receiving a grant of land in East Lothian. Throughout the centuries the name went through several spelling variations before Seton was finally adopted.*

MACBETH SITS AT A TABLE DEEP IN GLOOMY THOUGHT. HORRIBLE HALLUCINATIONS START. THIS TIME OF A DAGGER FLOATING BEFORE HIS FACE - THE KING'S DAGGER.

> *Note: This is Macbeth's third soliloquy.*

MACBETH (CONT'D)	**MACBETH**
What's this I see? A dagger floating in the air? The handle towards me? Come, let me hold you.	Is this a dagger which I see before me, The handle toward my hand? Come, let me clutch thee.

MACBETH STANDS AND GRABS AT NOTHING, BUT THE DAGGER NOW APPEARS TO HAVE JUMPED FORWARD TOWARDS HIS QUEST.

MACBETH (CONT'D)
I can't touch you, yet I can still see you!
Are you a deathly image that can be seen
but not held? Or are you just a product
of my overheated brain?

MACBETH
I have thee not, and yet I see thee still!
Art thou not, fatal vision, sensible
To feeling as to sight? Or art thou but
A dagger of the mind, a false creation,
Proceeding from the heat-oppressed brain?

HE LOOKS AWAY, AND THEN BACK AGAIN. IT IS STILL THERE BUT
IT HAS MOVED AGAIN TOWARDS KING DUNCAN'S ROOM.

MACBETH (CONT'D)
I still see you.

MACBETH
I see thee yet,

MACBETH STEPS TOWARDS THE VISION AND
DRAWS HIS OWN DAGGER TO COMPARE IT.

MACBETH (CONT'D)
As solid looking as my own here.
(*nervous*) You point me towards my
quest, and you are the instrument I
planned to use.
(*doubtful now*) Either my eyes deceive
my other senses, or they are the only
sense now working.

MACBETH
in form as palpable
As this which now I draw.
Thou marshall'st me the way that I was going,
And such an instrument I was to use.
Mine eyes are made the fools o' the other senses,
Or else worth all the rest.

HE CLOSES HIS EYES AND OPENS THEM AGAIN.

THE DAGGER IS STILL THERE. AGAIN IT HAS MOVED CLOSER TO HIS
INTENDED TARGET, ONLY THIS TIME, BLOOD IS DRIPPING FROM IT.

IT POINTS AND LEADS THE WAY TO HIS BLOODY DEED.

MACBETH (CONT'D)
Still I see you! With clots of blood on
your blade and handle that weren't
there before.

MACBETH
I see thee still,
And on thy blade and dudgeon, gouts of blood,
Which was not so before.

HE PUTS HIS OWN DAGGER OVER HIS EYES.

IN THE BACKGROUND ON AN UPPER LEVEL, LADY MACBETH SCAMPERS
BACK TO HER ROOM, EMPTY GOBLET IN HAND, UNSEEN BY MACBETH. SHE
PAUSES BRIEFLY, TAKING IN THE SIGHT OF MACBETH STANDING WITH HIS
DAGGER OVER HIS EYES, THEN WITH THE LOOK OF A WIFE WHO HAS SEEN
IT ALL BEFORE, CARRIES ON.

MACBETH (CONT'D)
I'm imagining it; it's the thought of the
bloody deed making my eyes see these
things.

MACBETH
There's no such thing:
It is the bloody business which informs
Thus to mine eyes.

Act II Scene I. Castle Courtyard. Night.

HE REMOVES HIS DAGGER FROM BEFORE HIS EYES AND SEES THE
VISION STILL THERE. HE TRIES TO MAKE SENSE OF IT.

MACBETH (CONT'D)
Right now, in half the world, the living seem dead, and wicked dreams plague blind sleep. Witches celebrate the goddess of the moon...

MACBETH
Now o'er the one half-world
Nature seems dead, and wicked dreams abuse
The curtain'd sleep; witchcraft celebrates
Pale Hecate's offerings;

HE PAUSES AS A WOLF HOWLS IN THE DISTANCE.

MACBETH (CONT'D)
...and old withered Murder - aroused by the howl of his sentinel, the wolf - with the stealthy pace and lustful strides of Tarquin, moves ghostlike through the night towards his victim.

MACBETH
and wither'd Murder,
Alarum'd by his sentinel, the wolf,
Whose howl's his watch, thus with his stealthy pace,
With Tarquin's ravishing strides, towards his design
Moves like a ghost.

Literary Note: Tarquin took his steps towards Lucretia to ravish her. Her rape by the Etruscan king's son and consequent suicide were responsible for the revolution which overthrew the monarchy and established the Roman Republic. Shakespeare often made references to classic literature, pandering to the educated audience members and nobility.

Note: Shakespeare wrote a poem about the Rape of Lucrece. He was grammar school educated only, in a time when playwrights were typically educated in top universities. They looked down on him and he frequently demonstrated his familiarity of classic literature, possibly to show he was equally capable.

Though Shakespeare left grammar school aged 14, the level of education was far higher then than today. The school days were long and arduous with up to twelve hours of studying. This puts into context the amount of work that Shakespeare churned out. He had been brought up and conditioned to working diligently for many hours, it explains his substantial knowledge of classic literature and history, and the extensive vocabulary for one leaving school so young by today's standards.

HIS MIND IS NOW MADE UP.

MACBETH (CONT'D)
Oh, sure and firm ground, muffle the direction of my steps. I fear your stones will announce my approach and break the ghostly silence best suited to my terrible deed.

MACBETH
Thou sure and firm-set earth,
Hear not my steps, which way they walk, for fear
Thy very stones prate of my whereabout,
And take the present horror from the time,
Which now suits with it.

MACBETH (CONT'D)	MACBETH
While I threaten to act, he still lives. Hot headed words lend themselves to cold feet.	Whiles I threat, he lives; Words to the heat of deeds too cold breath gives.

A SMALL BELL RINGS TWICE, SLOW AND DELIBERATE.

MACBETH (CONT'D)	MACBETH
The bell summons me. Time to get it over and done with. *Don't hear it, Duncan, for it is the bell, That summons you to heaven – or to hell.*	I go, and it is done: the bell invites me. *Hear it not, Duncan, for it is a knell That summons thee to heaven, or to hell.*

HE HEADS UP THE STAIRS TOWARDS DUNCAN'S QUARTERS
QUICKLY AND QUIETLY.

Note: Earlier, Lady Macbeth had told Macbeth to "leave the greater business to me". Now it is Macbeth who is carrying out the deed. Later on Lady Macbeth explains that she would have carried out the deed, but the King reminded her of her father so she couldn't do it. Quite when the plans were changed is not clear, she certainly has had no opportunity since putting the king to bed as Macbeth is awaiting her return to signify the King is in bed and that he and his attendants are drugged.

ACT II SCENE II

CASTLE BEDCHAMBER. NIGHT.

LADY MACBETH IS ALONE IN HER ROOM GULPING WINE, NERVOUSLY
PACING, LOOKING OUT TOWARDS KING DUNCAN'S QUARTERS EVERY TIME
SHE REACHES THE WINDOW. SHE LOOKS AT HER DRINK.

LADY MACBETH	LADY MACBETH
That which has made them drunk has made me bold. That which doused their spark has lit my fire...	That which hath made them drunk hath made me bold; What hath quench'd them hath given me fire.

SHE PAUSES AT THE OPEN WINDOW HEARING A SLIGHT SOUND.
SHE IS JUMPY

LADY MACBETH (CONT'D)	LADY MACBETH
What was that...	Hark!

AN OWL SCREECHES CLOSE BY, VERY LOUDLY, SUDDENLY FLAPPING AS IT
TAKES FLIGHT. SHE JUMPS AND SQUEALS, THEN SHUSHES HERSELF AND THE
OWL.

The hoot of an owl was considered an evil omen, signifying impending death for someone. Shakespeare calls it the "fatal bellman" as it was the bellman's job to ring the church bell when a person was near death. This enabled all who heard it to pray for the dying person. After the death, there would be a short peal, the way it was played would determine whether the dead soul was male or female. In this case the owl screeched for the death of King Duncan.

LADY MACBETH (CONT'D)	LADY MACBETH
(*shrieks*) Ah!.. Shhhh!... It was an owl shrieking, the messenger of death announcing the harshest good-night. He must be doing it now. The way is clear, his aides are drunk and I've drugged their drinks. They won't wake, they're dead to the world, their snoring won't protect him.	Peace! It was the owl that shriek'd, the fatal bellman, Which gives the stern'st good-night. He is about it: The doors are open, and the surfeited grooms Do mock their charge with snores: I have drugg'd their possets, That death and nature do contend about them, Whether they live or die.

A DISTANT OWL SCREECHES AGAIN.

MACBETH'S VOICE IS HEARD IN THE DISTANCE.

MACBETH
(*calling out, alarmed*)
Who's there? Who's that?

MACBETH
(*within*) Who's there? what, ho!

LADY MACBETH
Oh no, I fear they've awoken and it's not done! The attempt and not the deed will be our undoing. – What was that!

LADY MACBETH
Alack, I am afraid they have awaked
And 'tis not done. The attempt and not the deed
Confounds us. Hark!

SHE LISTENS... SHE HEARS A DISTANT MALE EXCLAMATION.

ANXIETY OVERWHELMS HER. SHE GULPS MORE WINE.

LADY MACBETH (CONT'D)
I left the daggers ready, he could not miss them. Had he not looked so like my father as he slept, I'd have done it myself.

LADY MACBETH
I laid their daggers ready;
He could not miss 'em. Had he not resembled
My father as he slept, I had done't.

FOOTSTEPS APPROACH. SHE LOOKS FEARFULLY AT THE DOOR.

THE DOOR OPENS AND MACBETH PLUNGES INTO THE ROOM, TWO BLOODIED DAGGERS IN HIS HAND.

LADY MACBETH (CONT'D)
My husband!

LADY MACBETH
My husband!

MACBETH
I've done the deed. Did you hear a noise?

MACBETH
I have done the deed. Didst thou not hear a noise?

HE THROWS THE DAGGERS DOWN BESIDE HIS WASH BASIN.

> Note: If the daggers and Macbeth's hands had been dripping blood as the text later suggests, the trail would have led back to Macbeth's chamber. We shall assume they were blood-stained, not dripping.

LADY MACBETH
Only an owl scream and the sounds of the night...

LADY MACBETH
I heard the owl scream and the crickets cry.

THERE IS AN ODD SOUND. THEY BOTH LISTEN...

LADY MACBETH (CONT'D)
Did you say something?

LADY MACBETH
Did not you speak?

MACBETH
When?

MACBETH
When?

LADY MACBETH
Just now.

LADY MACBETH
Now.

MACBETH	MACBETH
As I returned?	As I descended?
LADY MACBETH	LADY MACBETH
Yes.	Ay.

MACBETH HEARS THE VERY FAINT INDISTINCT SOUND OF GHOSTLY VOICES
IN THE AIR, CALLING HIS NAME, AS IF ACCUSING HIM.

MACBETH	MACBETH
Listen!	Hark!

THEY LISTEN, HEARING NOTHING, BOTH TWITCHY.

MACBETH (CONT'D)	MACBETH
Who's in the second bedroom?	Who lies i' the second chamber?
LADY MACBETH	LADY MACBETH:
His youngest, Donalbain.	Donalbain.

MACBETH LOOKS DOWN AT HIS BLOOD-DRENCHED HAND. HE LIFTS IT INTO
THE LIGHT OF THE CANDLE, SLOWLY TURNING IT, EXAMINING IT.

MACBETH	MACBETH
(*To his hand*) What a sorry sight.	This is a sorry sight.
LADY MACBETH	LADY MACBETH
(*scornfully*) A sorry sight? Foolish thing to say!	A foolish thought, to say a sorry sight.

MACBETH THINKS BACK ON WHAT HE'D DONE. AS HE HAD WALKED PAST
THE PRINCE'S ROOM, DONALBAIN (THE YOUNGEST PRINCE) LAUGHED IN
HIS SLEEP, THIS WOKE MALCOLM WHO OPENED HIS EYES SUDDENLY AS IF
FROZEN BY FEAR, AND SAT UP CALLING OUT, 'MURDER!'.

MACBETH	MACBETH
One of them laughed in their sleep, the other called out '*Murder!*'. They woke each other up.	There's one did laugh in's sleep, and one cried, "*Murder!*" That they did wake each other:

DONALBAIN, IN TURN WOKEN BY HIS BROTHER'S CRY, SAT UP ABRUPTLY
CLUTCHING HIS DAGGER. THE BROTHERS LOOKED AT EACH OTHER
FEARFULLY FOR A MOMENT BEFORE RECITING A PRAYER TOGETHER.
MALCOLM FINISHED THE PRAYER WITH, 'GOD BLESS US'. DONALBAIN
REPLIED, 'AMEN'. THEY CROSSED THEMSELVES BEFORE LAYING BACK
DOWN TO SLEEP.

MACBETH (CONT'D)	MACBETH
I stood and listened, but they just said their prayers and went back to sleep.	I stood and heard them: But they did say their prayers and address'd them Again to sleep.

LADY MACBETH

His sons both share the room.

MACBETH

One called out *"God bless us!"*, the other replied *"Amen"*.
(*looking at his hands*) As if they'd seen me with these blood stained hands.

LADY MACBETH

There are two lodged together.

MACBETH

One cried, *"God bless us!"* and *"Amen"* the other,
As they had seen me with these hangman's hands.

> Note: Here Shakespeare says "hands". Elsewhere it is only one hand that is blood stained. This may have been due to printer's errors.

LADY MACBETH LOOKS AT HIM, CONCERNED.

MACBETH (CONT'D)

Listening to their prayer, I could not bring myself to say *'Amen'* when they said *'God Bless Us'*.

MACBETH

List'ning their fear, I could not say *"Amen,"*
When they did say *"God bless us."*

LADY MACBETH

Stop dwelling on it.

LADY MACBETH

Consider it not so deeply.

MACBETH

But why couldn't I say *'Amen'*? I was in desperate need of a blessing, and *'Amen'* stuck in my throat.

MACBETH

But wherefore could not I pronounce *"Amen"*?
I had most need of blessing, and *"Amen"*
Stuck in my throat.

LADY MACBETH

The deed is done, stop thinking about it like this, we'll both be driven mad...

LADY MACBETH

These deeds must not be thought
After these ways; so, it will make us mad.

> Important Note: In Shakespeare's day, the King was believed to be a divine being, appointed by God, who had special powers no mortal man had. Killing the King was akin to damning your soul, almost like killing a part of God. Macbeth knew this very well as did audiences of the time.
>
> Knowing he has damned his soul for eternity, Macbeth can no longer bring himself to join in the prayer by saying 'Amen', the line uttered at the end of each prayer literally meaning 'so be it', or in simple terms, 'I agree'.

MACBETH INTERRUPTS HIS WIFE WITH A TERRIFIED QUESTIONING LOOK AS HE HEARS MORE ETHEREAL VOICES (WITCHES) IN THE AIR.

LADY MACBETH DOES NOT HEAR THEM.

VOICES

(*ethereal*) Sleep no more... Macbeth doth murder sleep...

> Note: Shakespeare didn't write a line for the voices, instead Macbeth describes the voices he hears. The audience then knows only Macbeth hears them.

MACBETH
I thought I heard a voice call, *"Sleep no more! Macbeth murders sleep".* Innocent sleep, sleep that mends the tangled cares of each dying day, sleep which bathes our aches, soothes troubled minds, nourishes the soul, nature's great tonic...

LADY MACBETH
(*interrupting*) What do you mean?

VOICES
(*ethereal*) *Sleep no more...*

MACBETH
Me thought I heard a voice cry "*Sleep no more! Macbeth doth Murder sleep*"— the innocent sleep, Sleep that knits up the ravell'd sleave of care, The death of each day's life, sore labor's bath, Balm of hurt minds, great nature's second course, Chief nourisher in life's feast —

LADY MACBETH
What do you mean?

MACBETH FREEZES.

LADY MACBETH REACTS - HE IS BEGINNING TO SPOOK HER AS WELL.

MACBETH
Still it calls, *"Sleep no more!"* for all to hear...

MACBETH
Still it cried, "*Sleep no more!*" to all the house;

MACBETH STANDS, LOOKING AROUND WILDLY.

HIS WIFE LOOKS ON CONCERNED.

VOICES
(*ethereal*) *'Glamis has murdered sleep, so Cawdor shall sleep no more, Macbeth shall sleep no more'.*

MACBETH
"Glamis has murdered sleep, so Cawdor shall sleep no more, Macbeth shall sleep no more".

MACBETH
"*Glamis hath murdered sleep, and therefore Cawdor Shall sleep no more. Macbeth shall sleep no more.*"

LADY MACBETH STANDS, CONCERNED FOR MACBETH'S MENTAL STATE.

Important Note: From this point Macbeth will not sleep and go slowly mad.

LADY MACBETH
Who is calling this? My noble Lord, your strength will be undone with such demented thoughts. Get some water and wash this foul evidence from your hands...

LADY MACBETH
Who was it that thus cried? Why, worthy Thane, You do unbend your noble strength, to think So brainsickly of things. Go, get some water And wash this filthy witness from your hand.

LADY MACBETH GLANCES AT THE WASH BOWL AND IS SHOCKED TO SEE THE BLOODIED DAGGERS BESIDE THE BOWL.

LADY MACBETH (CONT'D)

(*horrified*) Why did you bring the daggers here! They should have stayed there. Take them back and smear the sleeping guards with his blood.

LADY MACBETH

Why did you bring these daggers from the place?
They must lie there. Go, carry them, and smear
The sleepy grooms with blood.

MACBETH PICKS UP THE DAGGERS AS IF THEY ARE
SOMETHING FEARFUL TO HIM.

MACBETH

I daren't go back, I'm afraid to think of what I've done, let alone look at it again.

MACBETH

I'll go no more:
I am afraid to think what I have done;
Look on't again I dare not.

LADY MACBETH

(*holding out her hand*) Can't finish the job! Give me the daggers.

LADY MACBETH

Infirm of purpose!
Give me the daggers.

MACBETH, UNABLE TO MOVE, LOOKS HELPLESSLY AT HER.

SHE SNATCHES THE DAGGERS FROM HIM.

LADY MACBETH (CONT'D)

(*scornful*) The sleeping and the dead are just like pictures. Only a child fears a painting of the devil. If he still bleeds, I'll paint the faces of the guards. They must appear guilty.

LADY MACBETH

The sleeping and the dead
Are but as pictures; 'tis the eye of childhood
That fears a painted devil. If he do bleed,
I'll gild the faces of the grooms withal,
For it must seem their guilt.

LADY MACBETH LEAVES HURRIEDLY WITH THE DAGGERS.

MACBETH POURS WATER INTO HIS WASH BOWL AND PLUNGES HIS HANDS
IN, FRANTICALLY SCRUBBING. THE WATER TURNS RED.

THREE DEEP HARD KNOCKS ECHO THROUGHOUT THE CASTLE.

MACBETH FREEZES, FEARFUL AND CONFUSED. HE LOOKS UP TO THE
CEILING TRYING TO DETERMINE THE SOURCE OF THE SOUND.

MACBETH

What was that noise?

MACBETH:

Whence is that knocking?

HE LISTENS.

MACBETH (CONT'D)

What's wrong with me? I jump at every sound.

MACBETH

How is't with me, when every noise appals me?

HE HOLDS UP HIS HANDS. ONE IS STILL COVERED IN BLOOD AS BEFORE.

MACBETH (CONT'D)	MACBETH
Look at these hands. Ha! – Like Oedipus they'll pluck out my eyes for my crime.	What hands are here? Ha, they pluck out mine eyes!

> Note: The double meaning here is that he could not look on the scene again and the punishment for the crime. It also links to King Lear and King Oedipus, who both have their eyes plucked out for their crimes, Oedipus plucking out his own.

MACBETH THROWS THE BLOOD REDDENED BOWL WATER ONTO THE FIRE PRODUCING A LOUD HISS AND CLOUD OF STEAM.

HE REFILLS THE BOWL WITH FRESH WATER FROM A JUG.

MACBETH (CONT'D)	MACBETH
Is there enough water in all the world's oceans to wash my hand clean of all this blood? (*he pauses to look*) No, instead, this hand of mine will stain even the vast seas, turning the green to red.	Will all great Neptune's ocean wash this blood Clean from my hand? No, this my hand will rather The multitudinous seas incarnadine, Making the green one red.

LADY MACBETH RE-ENTERS THE ROOM AND WALKS TO MACBETH, HER BLOODIED HANDS HELD BEFORE HER.

LADY MACBETH	LADY MACBETH
It is done.	It is done.

SHE SEES HIM SCRUBBING HIS HANDS AND LOOKS AT HERS.

LADY MACBETH (CONT'D)	LADY MACBETH
Now my hands are the colour of yours...	My hands are of your color,...

SHE IS BITTER AT WHAT SHE SEES AS HIS LOSS OF NERVE AND FOR HAVING TO TAKE THE DAGGERS BACK HERSELF.

LADY MACBETH (CONT'D)	LADY MACBETH
...but I'd be ashamed to have a heart as white.	...but I shame To wear a heart so white.

LADY MACBETH WIPES THE BACK OF HER HAND ACROSS HER FACE.

SHE REALISES SHE HAS WIPED SOME BLOOD ON HER MOUTH AND CAN TASTE IT. HORRIFIED SHE SPITS AND PLUNGES HER FACE INTO THE WATER.

SHE SEES HER BLOOD SOAKED DRESS, SQUEALS IN ANGUISH AND RIPS IT OFF, THROWING IT INTO THE OPEN FIRE.

SHE SCRUBS HER HANDS FURIOUSLY, FRANTICALLY POURING FRESH WATER INTO HER BOWL AND SPLASHING IT OVER HER FACE. THEN SEEING THE WATER IS RED AGAIN SHE FRANTICALLY WIPES HER FACE WITH HER CLOTHING.

> Note: * Spoiler Alert * - *This action is related to a later scene where Lady Macbeth washes her hands constantly while sleepwalking.*

<u>THREE DEEP HARD KNOCKS</u>

THEY BOTH FREEZE.

LADY MACBETH	LADY MACBETH
Someone is knocking, at the South Entrance. We should go to our bedchamber.	I hear a knocking At the south entry. Retire we to our chamber.

LADY MACBETH REFILLS HER BOWL BEFORE
WASHING HER HANDS AND ARMS AGAIN.

LADY MACBETH (CONT'D)	LADY MACBETH
A little water will wash away the evidence. The hardest part is over.	A little water clears us of this deed: How easy is it then!

MACBETH IS STANDING STARING INTO SPACE WHILE MINDLESSLY WASHING
HIS HANDS. THEY BOTH CANNOT STOP WASHING THEIR HANDS.

SHE PAUSES, LOOKING AT HIM.

LADY MACBETH (CONT'D)	LADY MACBETH
Your resolve has abandoned you.	Your constancy Hath left you unattended.

<u>THREE DEEP KNOCKS</u> (MORE URGENT).

LADY MACBETH (CONT'D)	LADY MACBETH
Listen! More knocking.	Hark! more knocking:

MACBETH LOOKS UP AT NOTHING.

LADY MACBETH TEARS OFF HER CLOTHING TO PUT ON HER NIGHTGOWN.

SHE LOOKS AT MACBETH STILL STANDING THERE STARING.

LADY MACBETH (CONT'D)	LADY MACBETH
(*hisses*) Put on your nightgown in case someone comes and finds us out of bed... Stop dwelling on it so deeply!	Get on your nightgown, lest occasion call us And show us to be watchers. Be not lost So poorly in your thoughts.
MACBETH	MACBETH
I'd rather be lost in my thoughts than face what I've done.	To know my deed, 'twere best not know myself.

<u>THREE MORE DEEP KNOCKS</u>

Act II Scene II. Castle Bedchamber. Night.

MACBETH (CONT'D)

(*to the knocking*) Wake Duncan with your knocking! I wish you could!

MACBETH

Wake Duncan with thy knocking! I would thou couldst!

ACT II SCENE III

THE CASTLE MAIN GATE AT DAWN.

Note: The 'Porter scene' (as the first part of this scene is known) was put in as a break to enable the candles to be trimmed in the days before electric light and to offer some light comic relief. The part of the Porter would have been played by a comedy actor, bringing light relief and clown-like behaviour for the audience to enjoy in a break from the tension of the play, and allow the actor playing Macbeth time to clean the blood from his hands and change clothes. This scene includes biting satire regarding people and events in the news with a possible deeper message, the main theme here being the 'equivocator'.

Shakespeare wove direct references to the Gunpowder Plot into Macbeth because James I (the intended victim of a bomb attack) was in the audience for the first ever performance of Macbeth at Hampton Court Palace in 1606.

To commemorate the discovery of the treachery, King James had a medal created picturing a snake hiding amongst flowers. A reference to the medal is made when Lady Macbeth tells her husband to "look like the innocent flower, but be the serpent under it." The actual medal pictured can be seen in the British Museum in London.

Even more significant is an obvious allusion to the Jesuit priest, Father Henry Garnet, who had concealed his knowledge of the conspiracy. When Father Garnet finally confessed, he insisted that his previous perjury was not really perjury because he lied for God's sake. This completely turned around any religious thinking that had gone before. For this revolutionary bit of spin-doctoring he became known as the great "equivocator" and was hanged.

There is debate that there are underlying Catholic references in this play. Some scholars believe Shakespeare was a secret Catholic sympathizer in a day when Catholicism was banned. We know that Shakespeare's father was closely linked to the Gunpowder plot. The subject will not be explored here but there are many excellent works available on the subject.

OUTSIDE IN THE CASTLE COURTYARD A PORTER IS STAGGERING
DRUNKENLY OVER FLAGSTONES, HE HOLDS A BIG RING OF KEYS.

THREE LOUD KNOCKS ON THE CASTLE ENTRANCE DOORS.

HE STOPS AND LOOKS TOWARDS THE SOUND IN DRUNKEN ANNOYANCE.
HE LIFTS HIS KILT AND URINATES ON THE GROUND.

Note: Shakespeare does not mention urinating in this scene, it was added here as a stage direction to show the Porter was drunk, and to break up a long monologue. Directors can add any action they choose for dramatic effect.

A kilt or 'plaid' in Macbeth's time was more of a large cloak worn over a tunic.

The Porter's lines are in prose as he is a comic.

Act II Scene III. Castle Main Gate. Dawn.

PORTER

(*Drunk*) All this knocking! Even the gatekeeper at the gates of hell, would have worn out the key with so much knocking.

PORTER

Here's a knocking indeed!
If a man were porter of hell-gate, he should have old turning the key.

> Note: The 'Devil's porter' was mentioned in several Middle English works and would have been recognised by the audience as being the gatekeeper of Hell.

STILL URINATING, THE PORTER CARRIES OUT A PRETEND CONVERSATION AS IF AT THE GATES OF HELL. HE PLAYS ALL THE PARTS HIMSELF.

THREE LOUD KNOCKS

PORTER (CONT'D)

Knock, knock, knock!
(*as the devil*) In the name of Beelzebub, who's there?
(*as the announcer*) Here's a penniless farmer who hanged himself after gambling away his crop.
(*as devil*) Come right in! Bring plenty of handkerchiefs, here you'll be sweating for your sins.

PORTER

Knock, knock, knock!
Who's there, i' the name of Belzebub?
Here's a farmer that hanged himself on th' expectation of plenty.
Come in time! Have napkins enow about you; here you'll sweat for't.

> Note: 'Come in time' means literally come in quickly, don't wait around.

MORE KNOCKING

PORTER (CONT'D)

Knock, knock!
(*devil*) In the name of ...er... - some other devil's name - who's there?
(*announcer*) Here's an 'equivocating' man of God who could swear either side is true in the name of God, but the traitor could not swear his way into heaven by the same means.
(*devil*) Oh, do come in 'equivocator'!

PORTER

Knock, knock!
Who's there, in th' other devil's name?
Faith, here's an equivocator that could swear in both the scales against either scale, who committed treason enough for God's sake, yet could not equivocate to heaven.
O, come in, equivocator.

> Note: The 'equivocator' refers to the Jesuit Priest, Father Garnet, who had lied, or 'equivocated', in the name of God during the trial for the Gunpowder Plot. The audience would have known exactly who was being referred to.

HE FINISHES URINATING.

<u>MORE KNOCKING</u>

PORTER (CONT'D)	PORTER
(*in annoyance*) Knock, Knock, knock! (*devil*) Who's there? (*announcer*) Well, well, here's an English tailor, here for stealing cloth from tight fitting French breeches. (*devil*) Come in tailor. It's hot enough here to cook your goose iron.	Knock, knock, knock! Who's there? Faith, here's an English tailor come hither for stealing out of a French hose. Come in, tailor; here you may roast your goose.

> Note: Tailors would steal cloth from loose fitting breeches, but French hose was tight. Not only was the tailor found out, he was an idiot. The penalty for theft was public hanging.
>
> A 'goose' was the tailor's hot iron for pressing garments. Shakespeare puns on the word 'goose' as a bird you cook, and an iron you heat. 'His goose is cooked' means he is done for.

IT IS BEGINNING TO GET LIGHT. A RIVER OF URINE SHOWS ON THE GROUND

<u>MORE KNOCKING</u>

PORTER (CONT'D)	PORTER
Knock, knock! – There's no peace! (*aloud to door*) Who's knocking?	Knock, knock! Never at quiet! What are you?

HE SHIVERS AT THE COLD
AND STOPS HIS PRETEND CONVERSATION.

PORTER (CONT'D)	PORTER
(*shivers*) This place is too cold for hell. I'll be devil's gatekeeper no longer.	But this place is too cold for hell. I'll devil-porter it no further.

HE STAGGERS TOWARDS THE GATE.

PORTER (CONT'D)	PORTER
I had planned to let in one from every upstanding profession that had taken the 'soft route' to the everlasting fires of hell.	I had thought to have let in some of all professions, that go the primrose way to the everlasting bonfire.

<u>KNOCKING</u> - MORE URGENT THIS TIME.

PORTER (CONT'D)	PORTER
I'm coming, I'm coming!	Anon, anon!

76

Act II Scene III. Castle Main Gate. Dawn.

THE PORTER OPENS THE DOOR.
HE HUMBLY HOLDS OUT HIS HAND FOR A TIP.

PORTER (CONT'D)
Pray, remember the gatekeeper, sir.

PORTER
I pray you, remember the porter.

MACDUFF COMES THROUGH THE GATE, REGAL AND NONE TO HAPPY. HE
KNOCKS AWAY THE HAND HELD OUT FOR A TIP. LENNOX FOLLOWS BEHIND.

MACDUFF
Did you go to bed so late, my friend, that you could not rise?

MACDUFF
Was it so late, friend, ere you went to bed,
That you do lie so late?

PORTER
Indeed, sir, we were partying till the second cock... (*bawdy pause*) and at three o'clock, drink, sir, gives rise to three things.

PORTER
Faith, sir, we were carousing till the second cock:
and drink, sir, is a great provoker of three things.

MACDUFF
What three things does drink especially give rise to?

MACDUFF
What three things does drink especially provoke?

PORTER
Well, sir, a glowing nose... sleep... and... pissing. And it gives rise to lust of course, sir... but it gives and it takes. It gives rise to the desire, but takes away the performance.

PORTER
Marry, sir, nose-painting, sleep, and urine. Lechery, sir, it provokes and unprovokes: it provokes the desire, but it takes away the performance.

MACDUFF AND LENNOX LAUGH AT THE BAWDINESS. HAVING FOUND THEIR
LEVEL OF HUMOUR THE PORTER CONTINUES THE SUBJECT MATTER.

PORTER (CONT'D)
So yes, too much drink may be said to be the *equivocator* of lust. It makes him and it breaks him. It turns him on, it turns him off. It encourages him, then disheartens him, makes him stand up, then stand down. In short, it 'equivocates' his mind, causing him to lie, then leaves him lying there in his own piss.

PORTER
Therefore much drink may be said to be an equivocator with lechery: it makes him, and it mars him; it sets him on and it takes him off; it persuades him and disheartens him; makes him stand to and not stand to; in conclusion, equivocates him in a sleep, and giving him the lie, leaves him.

Note: Again, allusions to the priest lying under oath, mixed with bawdy banter.

MACDUFF SNIFFS THE AIR.

77

MACDUFF	MACDUFF
(*sniffing*) I believe drink left you lying last night.	I believe drink gave thee the lie last night.

PORTER	PORTER
That it did, sir, by the throat it grabbed me. But I got the better of him for his lie. I was too strong for him, even though he took my legs from under me at times, I beat him by throwing him up.	That it did, sir, i' the very throat on me: but I requited him for his lie, and, I think, being too strong for him, though he took up my legs sometime, yet I made a shift to cast him.

> Note: *"Shift to cast him": He is joking about wrestling with the drink. The drink took his legs from under him, but he made an evasive action (old meaning of shift) to throw him (cast), punning on vomiting, and on throwing someone. He also puns again on the word 'lie' – drink making you tell lies, and making you lie down when you've had too much, as well as referring again to the Priest.*

MACDUFF	MACDUFF
(*having heard enough*) Is your master up yet?	Is thy master stirring?

MACBETH COMES HURRIEDLY TOWARDS THE DOOR AS IF STILL DRESSING.

MACDUFF (CONT'D)	MACDUFF
Ah! Our knocking has woken him, here he comes now.	Our knocking has awaked him; here he comes.

LORD LENNOX	LENNOX
Good morning, noble sir.	Good morrow, noble sir.

MACBETH	MACBETH
Good morning to you both.	Good morrow, both.

MACDUFF	MACDUFF
Has the King risen, my worthy Lord?	Is the King stirring, worthy Thane?

MACBETH	MACBETH
Not yet, Macduff.	Not yet.

MACDUFF	MACDUFF
He ordered I call him at an early hour. (*sarcastic*) I have almost missed that hour.	He did command me to call timely on him; I have almost slipp'd the hour.

MACBETH	MACBETH
I'll take you to him.	I'll bring you to him.

MACBETH, MACDUFF, AND LENNOX WALK INTO THE COURTYARD.
IT IS NOW THE LIGHT OF DAWN.

Act II Scene III. Castle Main Gate. Dawn.

MACDUFF

I know hosting the King is a joyful occasion, Macbeth, but still a mighty inconvenience to you.

MACBETH

The delight we take eases the pain, Macduff.

MACDUFF

I know this is a joyful trouble to you;
But yet 'tis one.

MACBETH

The labor we delight in physics pain.

HE STOPS WALKING AND PLACES HIS HAND ON THE DOOR HANDLE.

MACBETH (CONT'D)

This is his quarters.

MACBETH

This is the door.

MACDUFF RESTRAINS MACBETH.

MACDUFF

I'll make so bold as to call him. It is my duty after all.

MACDUFF

I'll make so bold to call,
For 'tis my limited service.

MACBETH STEPS ASIDE, GESTURING THE WAY.

MACDUFF OPENS THE DOOR AND CLIMBS THE STAIRS TO THE KING'S
CHAMBER. MACBETH AND LENNOX WAIT AT THE DOOR BELOW.

LORD LENNOX

Does the King leave today, Macbeth?

LENNOX

Goes the King hence today?

MACBETH

He does, Lennox... or so he planned.

MACBETH

He does: he did appoint so.

LORD LENNOX

It was an unruly night. Where we slept, the chimneys were blown down. People said they heard wailing on the wind, screams of death, and hideous voices warning of turmoil and unrest to come in these already troubled times. An owl screeched the whole night long. Some say the earth tremored and shook.

LENNOX

The night has been unruly. Where we lay,
Our chimneys were blown down, and, as they say,
Lamentings heard i' the air, strange screams of
 death,
And prophesying with accents terrible
Of dire combustion and confused events
New hatch'd to the woeful time. The obscure bird
Clamor'd the livelong night. Some say the earth
Was feverous and did shake.

MACBETH

It was a rough night.

MACBETH

'Twas a rough night.

LORD LENNOX

In my short lifetime I can remember nothing like it.

LENNOX

My young remembrance cannot parallel
A fellow to it.

MACDUFF RUSHES OUT VISIBLY SHAKEN.

MACDUFF

Oh horror, horror, horror! No words could describe, nor mind conceive such horror!

MACBETH

What's happened?

LORD LENNOX

What's the matter, Macduff?

MACDUFF

Destruction on the grandest scale! The most sacrilegious murder has smashed open God's appointed leader, and robbed him of his sacred life.

MACBETH

What are you saying? Sacred life?

LORD LENNOX

You mean his Majesty?

MACDUFF

Go to his room, destroy your sight with this Gorgon horror. Ask me no more. Go see for yourselves.

MACDUFF

O horror, horror, horror! Tongue nor heart Cannot conceive nor name thee.

MACBETH

What's the matter?

LENNOX

What's the matter?

MACDUFF

Confusion now hath made his masterpiece. Most sacrilegious Murder hath broke ope The Lord's anointed temple and stole thence The life o' the building.

MACBETH

What is't you say? the life?

LENNOX

Mean you his Majesty?

MACDUFF

Approach the chamber, and destroy your sight With a new Gorgon. Do not bid me speak; See, and then speak yourselves.

Note: A Gorgon is a mythical creature which turns any onlooker to stone, the most famous being Medusa who had hair made of snakes.

MACBETH AND LENNOX RUSH UP THE STAIRS.

MACDUFF SHOUTS TO WAKE THE CASTLE,
HAMMERING ON ANY CLOSED DOORS.

MACDUFF (CONT'D)

Wake up! Wake up! Ring the alarm bell. Murder! Treason! Banquo! Donalbain! Malcolm! Wake up! Shake off your deep sleep, your false death, and look upon real death itself. Rise! Rise! And see what judgement day looks like! Malcolm! Banquo! Rise up from your graves like the walking dead on doomsday itself, and behold this horror. Sound the alarm!

MACDUFF:

Awake, awake!
Ring the alarum bell. Murder and treason!
Banquo and Donalbain! Malcolm, awake!
Shake off this downy sleep, death's counterfeit,
And look on death itself! Up, up, and see
The great doom's image! Malcolm! Banquo!
As from your graves rise up, and walk like sprites,
To countenance this horror! Ring the bell.

A SERVANT RUNS TO THE BELL TOWER AND STARTS RINGING THE BELL.

Act II Scene III. Castle Main Gate. Dawn.

LADY MACBETH STRIDES OUT DETERMINEDLY IN HER NIGHT GOWN. SHE HAS NOT PUT A DRESSING GOWN OVER IT. THIS IS A RUSE TO DISTRACT AS MUCH ATTENTION AWAY FROM THE MURDER AS POSSIBLE. THE GOWN APPEARING SEMI SEE-THROUGH IN THE EARLY DAYLIGHT.

SCREAMING MALE VOICES (THE KING'S ATTENDANTS WAKING AS MACBETH KILLS THEM) ADD TO THE CONFUSION.

LADY MACBETH	LADY MACBETH
What's going on!	What's the business,
Such a loud trumpeting rousing our sleeping guests? Speak, what is it!	That such a hideous trumpet calls to parley The sleepers of the house? Speak, speak!

BANQUO ENTERS, HEADING TOWARDS LADY MACBETH STILL THROWING ON HIS CLOTHES.

MACDUFF CALLS DOWN FROM THE UPPER LEVEL TO LADY MACBETH.

MACDUFF	MACDUFF
Oh, gentle lady, what I have to say is not for you to hear. The repetition of it in a woman's ear would be murder in itself.	O gentle lady, 'Tis not for you to hear what I can speak: The repetition in a woman's ear Would murder as it fell.

MACDUFF SEES BANQUO AND CALLS OUT WHILST RUNNING DOWNSTAIRS TO THE COURTYARD.

MACDUFF (CONT'D)	MACDUFF
Oh Banquo, Banquo! Our royal master's been murdered!	O Banquo, Banquo! Our royal master's murdered.

LADY MACBETH ON HEARING THIS STARTS OVERACTING.

LADY MACBETH	LADY MACBETH
Please God, no! What, here in our house?	Woe, alas! What, in our house?
BANQUO	**BANQUO**
Too wicked for any house. – My dear Duff, I beg you, say you are mistaken, say it is not so.	Too cruel any where. Dear Duff, I prithee, contradict thyself, And say it is not so.

ROSS ARRIVES AS MACBETH AND LENNOX RETURN. ALL LOOK TO THEM FOR NEWS. MACBETH IS OVERACTING, AND HAS BLOODY HANDS AGAIN.

MACBETH

Had I died an hour before this happened, I'd have lived a blessed life, but from this instant, nothing is worth living for. All belief destroyed. Honour and dignity murdered, the wine of life consumed, leaving only the dregs in this world.

MACBETH

Had I but died an hour before this chance,
I had lived a blessed time; for from this instant
There's nothing serious in mortality:
All is but toys; renown and grace is dead;
The wine of life is drawn, and the mere lees
Is left this vault to brag of.

MALCOLM AND DONALBAIN ARRIVE.

PRINCE DONALBAIN

What is amiss?

DONALBAIN

What is amiss?

MACBETH

You are, Donalbain, and you Malcolm, though you don't know it. The spring, the head, the fountain of your bloodline is corked, the very source of it capped.

MACBETH

You are, and do not know't:
The spring, the head, the fountain of your blood
Is stopp'd; the very source of it is stopp'd.

MACDUFF

Your royal father's been murdered.

MACDUFF

Your royal father's murdered.

PRINCE MALCOLM

(looking at Macbeth's hands suspiciously) What? By whom!

MALCOLM

O, by whom?

LORD LENNOX

It seems it was his aides, your highness. Their hands and faces were smeared with blood, as were their daggers which we found unwiped on their pillows. They just stared into space like madmen, no man's life could be trusted with them.

LENNOX

Those of his chamber, as it seem'd, had done't:
Their hands and faces were all badged with blood;
So were their daggers, which unwiped we found
Upon their pillows:
They stared, and were distracted; no man's life
Was to be trusted with them.

MACBETH

(showing his hands) Oh, how I now regret my fury which made me kill them.

MACBETH

O, yet I do repent me of my fury,
That I did kill them.

MACDUFF

Why did you kill them, Macbeth?

MACDUFF

Wherefore did you so?

MACBETH

Who can be wise and confused, calm and furious, loyal and neutral all in the same instant? No man. My haste to exact violent revenge overtook my reasoning. Duncan lay there, covered in the most precious of garments, the royal blood, his wounds going against all that is natural, leading to his unnatural end. There lay the murderers, soaked in the colours of their deadly work, their daggers covered in the royal blood they were meant to protect. Who could hold back that has a loving heart, a heart with the courage to show one's love?

MACBETH

Who can be wise, amazed, temperate and furious,
Loyal and neutral, in a moment? No man:
The expedition of my violent love
Outrun the pauser reason. Here lay Duncan,
His silver skin laced with his golden blood,
And his gash'd stabs look'd like a breach in nature
For ruin's wasteful entrance: there, the murderers,
Steep'd in the colors of their trade, their daggers
Unmannerly breech'd with gore. Who could
  refrain,
That had a heart to love, and in that heart
Courage to make's love known?

Note: Now we use the term 'blue blood' for royalty, but then it was often called golden, (not to be confused with the rarest blood type, also called golden blood). It emphasises the contrast of the blood to his pale (silver) skin. The paler your skin, the more noble you were, as you did not need to work and be exposed to the sun.

Note: Macbeth killing the guards rather conveniently conceals evidence, dead men can't talk, and their blood masks any trace of Duncan's.

LADY MACBETH

(*pretending to swoon*) Help me away from here! I feel faint!

LADY MACBETH

Help me hence, ho!

MACDUFF

See to the lady.

MACDUFF

Look to the lady.

BANQUO CATCHES HER IN HIS ARMS, PREVENTING HER FALLING.

Note: Was there a fondness between Lady Macbeth and Banquo? She wasn't shy in using any means to obtain her goals. Macbeth may have suspected this or he would have revealed to her his plans to murder Banquo later rather than keep them a secret. After all, they had shared the biggest murder together, any other would be insignificant by comparison.

MALCOLM AND DONALBAIN SPEAK TOGETHER IN CONFIDENCE.

PRINCE MALCOLM

(*aside to Donalbain*) Why are we holding our tongues, Donalbain? This is our problem more than anyone's.

MALCOLM

(*aside to Donalbain*)
Why do we hold our tongues,
That most may claim this argument for ours?

PRINCE DONALBAIN

(*aside to Malcolm*) What can we say here, where hidden treachery may rush out and seize us too? We must leave, we can grieve later.

DONALBAIN

(*aside to Malcolm*) What should be spoken here, where our fate, Hid in an auger-hole, may rush and seize us? Let's away; our tears are not yet brew'd.

Note: Auger - a boring tool for making holes, suggesting a small hiding place.

PRINCE MALCOLM

(*aside to Donalbain*) And avenge our grief later.

MALCOLM

(*aside to Donalbain*) Nor our strong sorrow Upon the foot of motion.

BANQUO CALLS OUT TO SERVANTS.

BANQUO

Take the lady away!

BANQUO

Look to the lady:

MEN HELP A SHIVERING LADY MACBETH AWAY.

Note: The following lines can apply equally to the attire of Lady Macbeth and the murder of the King, as she is led away.

BANQUO (CONT'D)

And when we have clothed our semi-naked frailties that suffer exposure to both the cold and this horror, let us reconvene to investigate this most bloody piece of work. Fears and doubts distract us. In God's trust I place myself, and in his name vow to uncover and destroy this treasonous evil.

BANQUO

And when we have our naked frailties hid, That suffer in exposure, let us meet And question this most bloody piece of work To know it further. Fears and scruples shake us: In the great hand of God I stand, and thence Against the undivulged pretence I fight Of treasonous malice.

MACDUFF

And I too.

MACDUFF

And so do I.

ALL

And I.

ALL

So all.

MACBETH

Let us quickly dress for action, and meet in the great hall.

MACBETH

Let's briefly put on manly readiness And meet i' the hall together.

ALL

Agreed. Aye.

ALL

Well contented.

ALL EXIT EXCEPT THE PRINCES.

PRINCE MALCOLM

What will you do, Donalbain? Let's not join them. False sorrow is something a traitor finds easy to show. I'll head for England.

PRINCE DONALBAIN

Ireland for me. Separate we'll be safer. Here, daggers hide behind men's smiles. The closer related in blood they are, the closer to a bloody fate are we.

PRINCE MALCOLM

A murderous arrow has been released but not yet ended its flight. Our safest bet is to avoid its aim. To our horses and let us slip away without ceremony. *For where there is no mercy left, To steal away is lawful theft.*

MALCOLM

What will you do? Let's not consort with them: To show an unfelt sorrow is an office Which the false man does easy. I'll to England.

DONALBAIN

To Ireland, I; our separated fortune Shall keep us both the safer. Where we are There's daggers in men's smiles: the near in blood, The nearer bloody.

MALCOLM

This murderous shaft that's shot Hath not yet lighted, and our safest way Is to avoid the aim. Therefore to horse; And let us not be dainty of leave-taking, *But shift away. There's warrant in that theft Which steals itself when there's no mercy left.*

ACT II SCENE IV

MACBETH'S CASTLE LATER THAT MORNING.

LORD ROSS IS ALONE IN THE ROOM WHERE THE KING DIED, COLLECTING
THE KING'S BELONGINGS. THE WEATHER IS DULL AND OVERCAST.

A HOLY FATHER ENTERS (OLD MAN), SUMMONED FOR THE DEATH.

Note: This scene was a conversation between Ross and an Old Man, but for this
translation he has been made a Holy Father as it makes sense of the lines.

HOLY FATHER
During my seventy years on this earth
I've lived through dreadful times and
witnessed terrible things, but nothing
compares to the horrors of last night.

OLD MAN
Threescore and ten I can remember well:
Within the volume of which time I have seen
Hours dreadful and things strange, but this sore
 night
Hath trifled former knowings.

LORD ROSS
Aye, good father, the heavens are
troubled by man's actions and show
their displeasure. The clock says it's
day, yet darkness strangles the travels
of the sky's lamp. Has night returned or
does the day hide its face in shame,
allowing darkness to entomb the earth
when living light should be kissing it?

ROSS
Ah, good father,
Thou seest the heavens, as troubled with man's act,
Threaten his bloody stage. By the clock 'tis day,
And yet dark night strangles the travelling lamp.
Is't night's predominance, or the day's shame,
That darkness does the face of earth entomb,
When living light should kiss it?

HOLY FATHER
It's unnatural, like this terrible deed.
Only last Tuesday, a high circling
falcon, pride of the sky, was attacked
and killed by a mouse-hunting owl.

OLD MAN
'Tis unnatural,
Even like the deed that's done. On Tuesday last
A falcon towering in her pride of place
Was by a mousing owl hawk'd at and kill'd.

LORD ROSS
And, unbelievable but true, Duncan's
horses – beautiful, swift, finest of their
breed – turned wild, breaking their
stalls, kicking out, refusing to obey, as
if waging war against mankind.

ROSS
And Duncan's horses—a thing most strange and
certain—
Beauteous and swift, the minions of their race,
Turn'd wild in nature, broke their stalls, flung out,
Contending 'gainst obedience, as they would make
War with mankind.

HOLY FATHER
It's said they tore at each other, biting.

OLD MAN
'Tis said they eat each other.

Note: 'Eat', now spelled and pronounced 'ate'.

86

LORD ROSS	ROSS
That they did, to my amazement. I saw it with my own eyes.	They did so, to the amazement of mine eyes That look'd upon't.

MACDUFF WALKS IN.

LORD ROSS (CONT'D)	ROSS
Here comes the good Macduff. (*to Macduff*) How are things now, sir?	Here comes the good Macduff. How goes the world, sir, now?
MACDUFF	MACDUFF
(*pointing to the weather*) Can you not see, Ross?	Why, see you not?

ROSS THEN POINTS TO THE BLOODSTAINED EVIDENCE.

LORD ROSS	ROSS
Do we know who did this vile, bloody deed?	Is't known who did this more than bloody deed?
MACDUFF	MACDUFF
(*carefully choosing his words*) The men Macbeth killed.	Those that Macbeth hath slain.
LORD ROSS	ROSS
Rue the day! What could they hope to gain?	Alas, the day! What good could they pretend?
MACDUFF	MACDUFF
They must have been paid. The King's two sons, Malcolm and Donalbain, have fled, which puts them high in suspicion of being behind the deed.	They were suborn'd: Malcolm and Donalbain, the King's two sons, Are stol'n away and fled, which puts upon them Suspicion of the deed.
LORD ROSS	ROSS
Another act against nature! Pointless ambition, it serves only to destroy its own aims. So now it's most likely the sovereignty will go to Macbeth.	'Gainst nature still! Thriftless ambition, that wilt ravin up Thine own life's means! Then 'tis most like The sovereignty will fall upon Macbeth.
MACDUFF	MACDUFF
He's been elected already. He's gone to Scone to be crowned.	He is already named, and gone to Scone To be invested.
LORD ROSS	ROSS
Where is the King's body now?	Where is Duncan's body?
MACDUFF	MACDUFF
Borne to the Isle of Iona, sacred resting place of his forebears and guardian of their bones.	Carried to Colmekill, The sacred storehouse of his predecessors And guardian of their bones.

87

> *Note: Colmekill is Iona, an island off the west coast of Scotland. The name is derived from St. Columba (Columba's cell) who converted Scotland to Christianity and founded a monastery (cell) there. Considered a holy place, Forty-eight kings are buried there including the real Macbeth and Duncan.*

LORD ROSS	ROSS
Are you going to Scone, Macduff?	Will you to Scone?

MACDUFF	MACDUFF
No, cousin, home to Fife for me.	No, cousin, I'll to Fife.

> *Note: A mark of his feelings. Not attending will be seen as a deliberate insult.*
>
> *The real Macduff was Thane of Fife. Today a ruined castle in Fife, known as Macduff's Castle, stands on the shoreline.*

LORD ROSS	ROSS
Well, I'd better head there.	Well, I will thither.

ROSS COLLECTS UP THE KING'S BELONGINGS PREPARING TO LEAVE.

MACDUFF	MACDUFF
Let's hope it goes well there. – Adieu, I fear the new rule will not be as easy as the old!	Well, may you see things well done there, Adieu, Lest our old robes sit easier than our new!

MACDUFF TURNS AND LEAVES.

LORD ROSS	ROSS
Farewell, father.	Farewell, father.

ROSS HEADS FOR THE DOOR WITH THE KING'S BELONGINGS.

HOLY FATHER	OLD MAN
God's blessing go with you and with those Who make good of evil, and friends of foes!	*God's benison go with you and with those That would make good of bad and friends of foes!*

> *Historic Note: Traditionally, Scottish kings were crowned at Scone where a large stone with a fascinating history was located. Known as the stone of destiny, its history (depending on which story you hear) dates back to biblical times. It was stolen by various nations before ending up in Scotland. Edward I removed the stone and brought it to England and had a throne built around it. Myth has it that monks guarding the original stone swapped it just before Edward stole it. Adding weight to this argument is the fact that the sandstone found locally around the village of Scone looks remarkably similar. It was returned to Scotland amidst great ceremony in 1996.*

End of Act II

ACT III

WHERE BLOODY DEEDS COME BACK TO HAUNT

WHAT'S DONE IS DONE

ACT III

ACT III SCENE I

THE KING'S PALACE AT FORRES. BANQUO'S QUARTERS.

MACBETH HAS BEEN KING A WHILE NOW.
BANQUO, A GUEST AT THE PALACE, IS PREPARING TO RIDE.

OUT OF THE WINDOW, BANQUO SEES MACBETH AND LADY MACBETH
HEADING ACROSS THE COURTYARD TOWARDS HIS QUARTERS. MACBETH IS
WEARING THE ROYAL ROBES AND CROWN LAST SEEN ON DUNCAN.

BANQUO
(*thinking out loud, watching Macbeth*)
You have it all now; King, Cawdor, Glamis. Everything. Just as the weird women predicted, though I fear you used foul means to get it. Yet they said it would not be handed down to your children, but that I, myself, would be the father of many Kings...
If they spoke the truth – as they have in your case, Macbeth – then why shouldn't they be my oracles too, and fortify me with hope?
(*admonishing self*) No, don't even think about it...

BANQUO
Thou hast it now: King, Cawdor, Glamis, all,
As the weird women promised, and I fear
Thou play'dst most foully for't: yet it was said
It should not stand in thy posterity,
But that myself should be the root and father
Of many kings. If there come truth from them—
As upon thee, Macbeth, their speeches shine—
Why, by the verities on thee made good,
May they not be my oracles as well
And set me up in hope? But hush, no more.

ROYAL TRUMPETS HERALD THE APPROACH OF THE KING.

MACBETH AND LADY MACBETH TOGETHER WITH ROSS AND LENNOX
WALK TOWARDS BANQUO'S ROOM.

THEY PAUSE FOR ATTENDANTS TO OPEN THE DOOR.

MACBETH
(*with some resentment*) Our chief guest.

LADY MACBETH
(*quietly to Macbeth*) If he had been forgotten, it would have left a suspicious gap at our great feast.

MACBETH
Here's our chief guest.

LADY MACBETH
If he had been forgotten,
It had been as a gap in our great feast
And all-thing unbecoming.

Act III Scene I. King's Palace at Forres.

THE DOORS OPEN AS MACBETH AND LADY MACBETH SWAGGER IN,
FOLLOWED BY LENNOX AND ROSS.

MACBETH SCANS THE ROOM AS IF LOOKING FOR EVIDENCE AGAINST
BANQUO. THE TWO MEN NOD IN ACKNOWLEDGEMENT.

*Note: Macbeth's relationship with Banquo has changed. He is now arrogant with
barely veiled sinister undertones to his conversation. He scans the room now as if
looking for evidence against Banquo, he doesn't trust or like him any more and he
is jealous. Especially as he believed that Banquo will provide his successor. Banquo
is as equally untrusting of Macbeth.*

MACBETH

Tonight, sir, we are holding a state banquet. I'll be requesting your presence.

BANQUO

Your highness's wish is my command, my duty to the crown is forever tied with an unbreakable bond.

MACBETH

Tonight we hold a solemn supper, sir,
And I'll request your presence.

BANQUO

Let your Highness
Command upon me, to the which my duties
Are with a most indissoluble tie
Forever knit.

MACBETH NODS HIS SILENT APPROVAL.

BANQUO DONS A RIDING COAT IN READINESS TO LEAVE.

MACBETH

You are riding out this afternoon?

BANQUO

Aye, your majesty.

MACBETH

Ride you this afternoon?

BANQUO

Ay, my good lord.

MACBETH PAUSES AS IF CONSIDERING THIS.

MACBETH

We would have desired your good advice at today's council meeting. It has always proved beneficial *in the past...* (*he pauses for effect*) ...but tomorrow will do. Are you riding far?

BANQUO

As far, my lord, as I can between now and supper. If my horse does not ride well, I may have to steal a couple of hours of night and return in the dark.

MACBETH

Do not miss our feast.

MACBETH

We should have else desired your good advice,
Which still hath been both grave and prosperous
In this day's council; but we'll take tomorrow.
Is't far you ride?

BANQUO

As far, my lord, as will fill up the time
'Twixt this and supper. Go not my horse the better,
I must become a borrower of the night
For a dark hour or twain.

MACBETH

Fail not our feast.

91

BANQUO
I will not, your majesty.

MACBETH
We hear our murdering cousins have taken refuge in England and Ireland. They have not confessed to their cruel parental murder, instead, they feed their supporters stories of wild invention. But more of that tomorrow, where we also have affairs of state craving our joint attention. – Now, to your horse. Adieu... until you return this evening.

BANQUO
My lord, I will not.

MACBETH
We hear our bloody cousins are bestow'd
In England and in Ireland, not confessing
Their cruel parricide, filling their hearers
With strange invention. But of that tomorrow,
When therewithal we shall have cause of state
Craving us jointly. Hie you to horse; adieu,
Till you return at night.

MACBETH HALF TURNS AND STOPS – AS IF IN SUDDEN AFTERTHOUGHT
BUT WITH DEVIOUS INTENTION.

MACBETH (CONT'D)
Your son, Fleance, rides with you?

BANQUO
Aye, your majesty, he awaits me.

MACBETH
Goes Fleance with you?

BANQUO
Ay, my good lord. Our time does call upon's.

A SLIGHT SMILE SPREADS ACROSS MACBETH'S FACE.

MACBETH
Then I wish you a good and comfortable ride. May your horses be swift and sure of foot. Farewell.

MACBETH
I wish your horses swift and sure of foot,
And so I do commend you to their backs.
Farewell.

MACBETH TURNS AND STARTS WALKING OUT.

LADY MACBETH FOLLOWS.

MACBETH STOPS OUTSIDE AND SPEAKS TO ALL GATHERED.

MACBETH (CONT'D)
Let everyman be free with his time until seven this evening. To make the company all the sweeter, we will keep to ourselves till suppertime. Until then... (*he pauses*) ... God be with you!

MACBETH
Let every man be master of his time
Till seven at night; to make society
The sweeter welcome, we will keep ourself
Till supper time alone. While then... God be with you!

THE LORDS GO THEIR OWN WAYS.

BANQUO PAUSES FOR A MOMENT WITHOUT TURNING, FEELING MACBETH'S
EYES BURNING INTO THE BACK OF HIM, THEN TURNS AND LEAVES.

MACBETH HEADS TOWARDS HIS STUDY, CALLING TO HIS ATTENDANT.

MACBETH (CONT'D)	MACBETH
Seton! A word with you.	Sirrah, a word with you.

THE ATTENDANT, (SETON) WAITING OUTSIDE, NODS. MACBETH ENTERS HIS STUDY, SETON FOLLOWS AND CLOSES THE DOOR.

Note: Again, for the translation, the Attendant has been named as Seton.

MACBETH (CONT'D)	MACBETH
(*said in quiet confidence*) Are the men waiting to see me?	Attend those men Our pleasure?
SETON	**SERVANT**
They are, your majesty, at the palace gates.	They are, my lord, without the palace gate.
MACBETH	**MACBETH**
Bring them to me.	Bring them before us.

SETON NODS ACKNOWLEDGEMENT, TURNS AND LEAVES.

Note: Macbeth now speaks his fourth soliloquy.

MACBETH (CONT'D)

(*aside*) To be King is easy, to remain King, not so, unless I take precautions. My fears in Banquo run deep. In his regal nature lies a royal ambition much to be feared. He's daring, but within that fearless temper lies the wisdom to guide his courage with caution. He's the only one I fear. In his company I feel uneasy, my guiding spirit leaves me, as Mark Anthony's did in Caesar's presence. He rebuked the witches when they first named me King, demanding they speak to *him*. Then prophet like, they announced *him* father to a line of kings, while on my head they placed a childless crown and put a barren sceptre in my hand, only for it to be wrenched from my grasp by some unrelated hand, no son of mine succeeding me.

MACBETH

To be thus is nothing,
But to be safely thus. - Our fears in Banquo
Stick deep, and in his royalty of nature
Reigns that which would be fear'd. 'Tis much he
  dares,
And, to that dauntless temper of his mind,
He hath a wisdom that doth guide his valor
To act in safety. There is none but he
Whose being I do fear; and under him
My genius is rebuked, as it is said
Mark Antony's was by Caesar. He chid the sisters,
When first they put the name of King upon me,
And bade them speak to him; then prophet-like
They hail'd him father to a line of kings:
Upon my head they placed a fruitless crown
And put a barren sceptre in my gripe,
Thence to be wrench'd with an unlineal hand,
No son of mine succeeding.

MACBETH PACES THE ROOM, AGITATED.

MACBETH (CONT'D)	MACBETH
If what they say is true, I have defiled myself for Banquo's descendants. Murdered the gracious Duncan for them. Removed my soul from its state of grace only for them. Sold my eternal soul to the Devil to make them kings! The seeds of Banquo, kings! I can not allow it. So, come, Fate, I challenge you, a duel to the death for my destiny!	If't be so, For Banquo's issue have I filed my mind, For them the gracious Duncan have I murdered, Put rancors in the vessel of my peace Only for them, and mine eternal jewel Given to the common enemy of man, To make them kings, the seed of Banquo kings! Rather than so, come, Fate, into the list, And champion me to the utterance!

> Note: The 'Fates' were three goddesses who determined a human's destiny, or fate. One spun (made) the thread of life, one decided its length, and one cut it.

THERE IS A KNOCK AT THE DOOR.

MACBETH (CONT'D)	MACBETH
Who's there?	Who's there?

THE DOOR OPENS. TWO MEN STAND THERE WITH SETON.

MACBETH BECKONS THEM IN.

MACBETH (CONT'D)	MACBETH
(*to Seton*) Seton, step outside and wait till I call you.	Now go to the door, and stay there till we call.

MACBETH WAITS UNTIL THE ATTENDANT LEAVES AND CLOSES THE DOOR.

MACBETH (CONT'D)	MACBETH
It was yesterday we spoke, wasn't it?	Was it not yesterday we spoke together?

1ST MURDERER	FIRST MURDERER
It was, if you please, your Highness.	It was, so please your Highness.

MACBETH	MACBETH
Well then, have you considered what I told you? That in the past it was '*him*' who treated you so poorly? You thought it had been my doing. I explained this to you in our last conversation. I went over the facts, offered proof, how you were deceived, the men and the means by which you were misled, and other facts to which even a halfwit or a madman would say, "It was Banquo".	Well then, now Have you consider'd of my speeches? Know That it was he, in the times past, which held you So under fortune, which you thought had been Our innocent self? This I made good to you In our last conference, pass'd in probation with you How you were borne in hand, how cross'd, the instruments, Who wrought with them, and all things else that might To half a soul and to a notion crazed Say, "Thus did Banquo."

94

1ˢᵀ MURDERER

You made it clear to us, yes.

MACBETH

I did indeed, and went further, which is the point of our second meeting. Is your nature so weak that you can just let this go? Are you so Christian that you'd pray for this *good* man and his descendants? A man whose heavy hand led you closer to an early grave and left your families impoverished forever?

1ˢᵀ MURDERER

We are men, your majesty.

MACBETH

Oh yes, you might come under the heading '*men*', in the way greyhounds, mongrels, spaniels, strays, retrievers or wolves all come under the heading, '*dogs*'. Catalogued in order of ability; the swift, the slow, the tracker, the guard, the hunter, each according to the gift that bounteous nature has bestowed upon him which stands him apart from others of the same name. The same is true of men. Now if you have a position in the ranks of mankind above the lowest, say so, and I'll put this business your way; the execution of which will remove your enemy and bring you closer to my heart, which is weakened while he lives, but in his demise would be restored to full health.

2ᴺᴰ MURDERER

I'm a man, your majesty, so incensed by the vile knocks and blows this world serves up that I care not what I do to spite the world.

1ˢᵀ MURDERER

And me. I'm so weary of the sufferings and misfortunes of life that I would risk mine on any chance to mend it, or be rid of it.

FIRST MURDERER

You made it known to us.

MACBETH

I did so, and went further, which is now
Our point of second meeting. Do you find
Your patience so predominant in your nature,
That you can let this go? Are you so gospell'd,
To pray for this good man and for his issue,
Whose heavy hand hath bow'd you to the grave
And beggar'd yours for ever?

FIRST MURDERER

We are men, my liege.

MACBETH

Ay, in the catalogue ye go for men,
As hounds and greyhounds, mongrels, spaniels, curs,
Shoughs, waterrugs, and demi-wolves are clept
All by the name of dogs. The valued file
Distinguishes the swift, the slow, the subtle,
The housekeeper, the hunter, every one
According to the gift which bounteous nature
Hath in him closed, whereby he does receive
Particular addition, from the bill
That writes them all alike; and so of men.
Now if you have a station in the file,
Not i' the worst rank of manhood, say it,
And I will put that business in your bosoms
Whose execution takes your enemy off,
Grapples you to the heart and love of us,
Who wear our health but sickly in his life,
Which in his death were perfect.

SECOND MURDERER

I am one, my liege,
Whom the vile blows and buffets of the world
Have so incensed that I am reckless what
I do to spite the world.

FIRST MURDERER

And I another
So weary with disasters, tugg'd with fortune,
That I would set my life on any chance,
To mend it or be rid on 't.

MACBETH

Both of you now know Banquo is your enemy.

BOTH:

We do / Yes, your highness.

MACBETH

He is mine too, and to such a bloody degree that every minute of his existence stabs at the very heart of me. And though I could sweep him from my sight using my royal powers and justify it as my wish, I cannot – on account of certain mutual friends he and I have whose favour I do not wish to lose. Instead I'll feign sorrow at the fall of the man I myself struck down. So, for this, and various other important reasons, I am seeking your assistance in concealing the truth from the public.

2ND MURDERER

We'll do whatever you command us, your majesty.

1ST MURDERER

Though our lives...

MACBETH

Both of you
Know Banquo was your enemy.

BOTH MURDERERS

True, my lord.

MACBETH

So is he mine, and in such bloody distance
That every minute of his being thrusts
Against my near'st of life: and though I could
With barefaced power sweep him from my sight
And bid my will avouch it, yet I must not,
For certain friends that are both his and mine,
Whose loves I may not drop, but wail his fall
Who I myself struck down. And thence it is
That I to your assistance do make love,
Masking the business from the common eye
For sundry weighty reasons.

SECOND MURDERER

We shall, my lord,
Perform what you command us.

FIRST MURDERER

Though our lives —

THE MURDERER PAUSES, SUGGESTING THEY WILL BE IN DANGER.

MACBETH CARRIES ON, DELIBERATELY IGNORING THE WORDS.

MACBETH

(*interrupting*) Your spirit does you proud. Within the hour I'll advise you *exactly* where to plant yourselves, and the time it is to be done.

MACBETH

Your spirits shine through you. Within this hour at
  most
I will advise you where to plant yourselves,
Acquaint you with the perfect spy o' the time,

MACBETH STANDS.

Note: 'Spy' - There is disagreement about the meaning behind the use of the word 'spy' in this line. The most common meaning at the time was look-out, observe or scout. Spies and spying (intelligence gathering) were not invented until Queen Elizabeth's time (it is believed Marlow, a contemporary of Shakespeare, was a spy in the employ of Walsingham, Elizabeth's spymaster), so here it probably means the perfect time and place to be for look-out duty.

MACBETH (CONT'D)

The moment is upon us, it must be done tonight, and some distance from the Palace, and remember always that I must be completely above suspicion – I want no clumsiness or botched work. – His son, Fleance, accompanies him...

MACBETH

The moment on 't; for 't must be done tonight, And something from the palace; always thought That I require a clearness; and with him — To leave no rubs nor botches in the work — Fleance his son, that keeps him company,

THE MEN LOOK TAKEN ABACK AT THIS.

MACBETH PAUSES AND LOOKS AT THEM COLDLY.

MACBETH (CONT'D)

His loss is no less important to me than his father's. He must share the same fate on that dark hour. Leave now, discuss whether you are both in agreement. I will join you soon.

MACBETH

Whose absence is no less material to me Than is his father's, must embrace the fate Of that dark hour. Resolve yourselves apart: I'll come to you anon.

THE TWO MURDERERS GLANCE AT EACH OTHER BEFORE ANSWERING.

2ND MURDERER

We are already decided, your majesty.

BOTH MURDERERS

We are resolved, my lord.

MACBETH

I'll call you shortly. Wait in my antechamber.

MACBETH

I'll call upon you straight. Abide within.

THE MURDERERS ARE USHERED INTO AN ADJOINING SIDE ROOM, SAFELY OUT OF SIGHT OF ANY PRYING EYES.

Note: Macbeth does not use direct words such as 'murder' or 'kill, etc. Nor does he mention payment directly. Payment was considered too lower class for Kings to be dealing with. People did the King's bidding without question. Macbeth only hints at murder, but he knows the men fully understand his meaning.

MACBETH (CONT'D)

(to self) And so it is done: Banquo, if your
    soul's flight,
Is to find heaven, it will find out tonight.

MACBETH

(to self)
It is concluded: Banquo, thy soul's flight,
If it find heaven, must find it out tonight.

MACBETH OPENS THE STUDY DOOR, HE NODS A SIGNAL OF AFFIRMATION TO THE ATTENDANT (SETON), WHO NODS BACK SHOWING HE UNDERSTANDS.

AS MACBETH HEADS OFF, SETON ENTERS THE STUDY AND HEADS FOR THE SIDE ROOM WHERE THE MURDERERS AWAIT.

ACT III SCENE II

KING'S PALACE AT FORRES. LATER ON.

LADY MACBETH IS ALONE IN HER THOUGHTS.

SHE HEARS HORSES LEAVE. SHE CALLS TO A SERVANT.

LADY MACBETH	LADY MACBETH
Has Banquo left the Palace?	Is Banquo gone from court?
SERVANT	SERVANT
Yes, Madam. He returns this evening.	Ay, madam, but returns again tonight.

LADY MACBETH PAUSES IN ANXIOUS THOUGHT.

LADY MACBETH	LADY MACBETH
Tell the King I wish to speak with him, when he can spare me a few words.	Say to the King I would attend his leisure For a few words.
SERVANT	SERVANT
I will, Ma'am.	Madam, I will.

THE SERVANT LEAVES.

LADY MACBETH	LADY MACBETH
(aside, anxious, reciting a rhyme)	*Nought's had, all's spent,*
Nothing is gained, everything's spent,	*Where our desire is got without content.*
When that we wished for brings no content.	*'Tis safer to be that which we destroy*
'Tis better to be that which we destroy	*Than by destruction dwell in doubtful joy.*
Than by its destruction live in false joy.	

MACBETH ENTERS DEEP IN HIS THOUGHTS, HE BARELY NOTICES HER.

SHE IS CONCERNED WITH HIS BEHAVIOUR. THE BALANCE OF POWER IN
THEIR MARRIAGE HAS ALREADY BEGUN TO TURN.

LADY MACBETH (CONT'D)	LADY MACBETH
What's the matter, my lord! Why do you keep to yourself with only your wretched thoughts for company? They should have died along with those they think of.	How now, my lord! Why do you keep alone, Of sorriest fancies your companions making, Using those thoughts which should indeed have died With them they think on?

MACBETH DOES NOT ANSWER. ANXIOUSLY SHE MOVES TO HIM.

LADY MACBETH (CONT'D)	LADY MACBETH
You should not dwell on things you cannot change. What's done is done.	Things without all remedy Should be without regard. What's done is done.

Note: "What's done is done". Contrary to popular belief, Shakespeare did not invent this expression. Its source was a translation of a 14th century French proverb, "When a thing is already done, it cannot be undone". However, Shakespeare's use of its English language version in Macbeth is one of the earliest recorded uses of it in print. Later on (Act 5 Scene 1) Lady Macbeth will say the line 'what's done cannot be undone' to contrast this line.

MACBETH	MACBETH
We have wounded the snake, not killed it. The wounds will heal. Our weak vengeance leaves us in danger of its renewed bite. But let the world fall apart, let heaven and earth collide, we'll not eat our meals in fear, nor endure the affliction of these terrible dreams that shake us nightly from our sleep. Better to be with the dead – whom we send to their peace to gain our peace – than to torture our minds with restless turmoil. Duncan lies in his grave, after the fitful fever of life he sleeps well. Treason has done its worst. No steel or poison, no rebel uprising, no foreign army, nothing, can touch him now.	We have scotch'd the snake, not kill'd it. She'll close and be herself, whilst our poor malice Remains in danger of her former tooth. But let the frame of things disjoint, both the worlds suffer, Ere we will eat our meal in fear and sleep In the affliction of these terrible dreams That shake us nightly. Better be with the dead, Whom we, to gain our peace, have sent to peace, Than on the torture of the mind to lie In restless ecstasy. Duncan is in his grave; After life's fitful fever he sleeps well; Treason has done his worst: nor steel, nor poison, Malice domestic, foreign levy, nothing, Can touch him further.
LADY MACBETH	**LADY MACBETH**
Come, my beloved. Take that grave look off your face. Tonight you must be bright and cheerful among our guests.	Come on, Gentle my lord, sleek o'er your rugged looks; Be bright and jovial among your guests tonight.
MACBETH	**MACBETH**
That I shall, my love. And so, I hope, will you. Remember to pay special attention to Banquo. Praise him with your eye and your tongue. These times are unsafe, we must protect ourselves with flattery. Let our faces mask what lies in our hearts.	So shall I, love, and so, I pray, be you: Let your remembrance apply to Banquo; Present him eminence, both with eye and tongue: Unsafe the while, that we Must lave our honors in these flattering streams, And make our faces vizards to our hearts, Disguising what they are.

Note: Macbeth knows Banquo will not be at the feast. Perhaps he wishes his wife's reaction to his absence to be genuine. "Unsafe the while, that we" is missing two feet (four syllables) – printer's error or was Macbeth interrupted?

LADY MACBETH	LADY MACBETH
You must stop this talk.	You must leave this.

MACBETH

Oh, scorpions plague my mind, dear wife, while Banquo and his son Fleance live!

LADY MACBETH

They only lease the form nature has given them, they're not immortal.

MACBETH

There's comfort in that; they can be dealt with. So be joyful. Before the bat has flown his rooftop haunt, before the goddess of darkness has summoned the black-winged beetle to fill the night with its drowsy hum, a deed of dire importance will be done.

LADY MACBETH

What will be done?

MACBETH

Stay ignorant of the deed, dearest one, till the time comes to celebrate it. Come, cover of darkness, blind the tender eye of pitiful day, and with your bloodied and invisible hand quash and tear to pieces that mortal tie which keeps me in bondage. Light grows dim, and the crow takes flight to the shadowy wood.
Good creatures of day do begin to drowse,
While night's black creatures to their prey do
  rouse.
You wonder at my words, but wait and see:
Evil breeds evil, and on itself feeds.

MACBETH

O, full of scorpions is my mind, dear wife!
Thou know'st that Banquo and his Fleance lives.

LADY MACBETH

But in them nature's copy's not eterne.

MACBETH

There's comfort yet; they are assailable.
Then be thou jocund. Ere the bat hath flown
His cloister'd flight; ere to black Hecate's summons
The shard-borne beetle with his drowsy hums
Hath rung night's yawning peal, there shall be
  done
A deed of dreadful note.

LADY MACBETH

What's to be done?

MACBETH

Be innocent of the knowledge, dearest chuck,
Till thou applaud the deed. Come, seeling night,
Scarf up the tender eye of pitiful day,
And with thy bloody and invisible hand
Cancel and tear to pieces that great bond
Which keeps me pale! Light thickens, and the
  crow
Makes wing to the rooky wood:
Good things of day begin to droop and drowse,
Whiles night's black agents to their preys do rouse.
Thou marvell'st at my words, but hold thee still:
Things bad begun make strong themselves by ill.

HE TURNS TO LEAVE.

Note: Macbeth refers to his wife in hawking terms: 'chuck' - alternative term for chick, 'seeling' - sewing the eyes of a hawk shut to keep it calm, 'scarf up' - the hawk's eyes were scarfed or hooded to stop it flying away.

MACBETH (CONT'D)

So dearest, come with me.

MACBETH

So, prithee, go with me.

Note: Macbeth could also mean, 'go along with my plans', however, he needs an alibi and possibly some company for moral support.

ACT III SCENE III

SOME DISTANCE FROM THE PALACE. DUSK.

THE TWO MURDERERS ARE WAITING BESIDE A TRACK AT DUSK.

A THIRD MAN RIDES UP BEHIND THEM TAKING THEM BY SURPRISE. HE
STOPS BEHIND THEM BUT DOESN'T DISMOUNT. IT IS SETON. SENT TO
ENSURE THEY COMPLETE THE DEADLY DEED.

*Note: The third man was simply called Third Murderer, but since Seton knew
about the murderers and Macbeth trusted him, it makes sense to make him the
man Macbeth would send to check the deed had been done. However, do not
quote this in exams. Alternatively, some scholars have argued that it was
Macbeth himself, but since he specifically stated he wished to distance himself
from the crime, and because he was eager to hear details later at the feast, this
makes little sense.*

1ST MURDERER	FIRST MURDERER
Why are you here? Who sent you?	But who did bid thee join with us?
SETON	THIRD MURDERER
Macbeth.	Macbeth.
2ND MURDERER	SECOND MURDERER
He need not distrust us. He gave us our orders, we know what we have to do down to the finest detail.	He needs not our mistrust, since he delivers Our offices and what we have to do, To the direction just.
1ST MURDERER	FIRST MURDERER
You'd better join us then. The sky glimmers with the last streaks of daylight. Now is the time the late traveller spurs his mount to reach the timely inn...	Then stand with us. The west yet glimmers with some streaks of day; Now spurs the lated traveller apace To gain the timely inn, and near approaches...
SETON	THIRD MURDERER
(*interrupting*) Listen! Horses.	Hark! I hear horses.
1ST MURDERER	FIRST MURDERER
...our subject approaches.	The subject of our watch.

BANQUO AND FLEANCE SLOW TO A CANTER ALONG THE TRACK, NEARING
A STABLING AREA A MILE FROM THE CASTLE.

*Note: Shakespeare had them walk the last mile to save bringing horses on stage.
Because of this, the characters explain occurrences rather than act them.*

BANQUO
(*off*) Hey there! Give us a light.

BANQUO
(*within*) Give us a light there, ho!

BANQUO AND FLEANCE DISMOUNT.

IT IS BECOMING DARK.

THEY HAND THEIR MOUNTS OVER TO THE STABLE HANDS.

2ND MURDERER
It must be him. The other invited guests are already inside the Palace.

SECOND MURDERER
Then 'tis he: the rest
That are within the note of expectation
Already are i' the court.

1ST MURDERER
They've dismounted.

FIRST MURDERER
His horses go about.

Note: "Go about" is a nautical term for a sailing ship changing to the opposite tack when sailing into wind, probably meaning the horses were being led off into the stabling area while the intended victims carried on by foot.

SETON
About a mile. That's normal, everyone does. They walk from here to the palace gate.

THIRD MURDERER
Almost a mile, but he does usually —
So all men do — from hence to the palace gate
Make it their walk.

BANQUO AND FLEANCE APPROACH WHERE THE MURDERERS ARE
SECRETED ON FOOT WITH A TORCH.

2ND MURDERER
(*whispered*) A light, a light!

SECOND MURDERER
A light, a light!

SETON
It's him.

THIRD MURDERER
'Tis he.

1ST MURDERER
Let's go.

FIRST MURDERER
Stand to't.

THE MURDERERS CALMLY STEP ONTO THE TRACK MEETING
BANQUO AND FLEANCE FACE TO FACE.

BANQUO
(*pleasantly*) There'll be rain tonight.

BANQUO
It will be rain tonight.

1ST MURDERER
Let it come down!

FIRST MURDERER
Let it come down.

Note: Punning on the word rain. Firstly, the blows rain down on Banquo making the blood rain down, secondly the reign of a line of kings from Banquo and the fall of the reign of Macbeth which this event helps trigger.

Act III Scene III. Some Distance From The Palace. Dusk.

THEY ATTACK BANQUO.

SETON WATCHES FROM BEHIND.

THE MURDERERS HACK AT BANQUO'S HEAD WITH A SMALL HATCHET AND
A KNIFE LEAVING AN OPPORTUNITY FOR FLEANCE TO ESCAPE.

BANQUO
Treachery! Run, Fleance! Flee, flee, flee!
You can revenge...
(*he is hit*) Uh, rogue!

BANQUO
O, treachery! Fly, good Fleance, fly, fly, fly!
Thou mayst revenge. O slave!

FLEANCE DROPS THE TORCH AND MAKES GOOD HIS ESCAPE.

MURDERER 1 STAMPS ON THE TORCH, EXTINGUISHING IT.

BANQUO DIES.

SETON SEES FLEANCE FLEEING JUST BEFORE IT SUDDENLY GOES DARK.

SETON
Who put out the light?

1ST MURDERER
Wasn't that the plan?

SETON
You only killed one! His son has fled.

2ND MURDERER
We've only done half the job.

THIRD MURDERER
Who did strike out the light?

FIRST MURDERER
Was't not the way?

THIRD MURDERER
There's but one down; the son is fled.

SECOND MURDERER
We have lost best half of our affair.

1ST MURDERER KICKS THE LIFELESS BODY OF BANQUO OVER SO THAT IT
ROLLS INTO A DITCH BESIDE THE ROAD OUT OF IMMEDIATE SIGHT.

1ST MURDERER
Let's get away from here and report
how much we have done.

FIRST MURDERER
Well, let's away and say how much is done.

ACT III SCENE IV

THE BANQUETING HALL OF THE PALACE A BANQUET.

A BANQUET IS PREPARED. THE LORDS ARE ALL GATHERED.

THE KING AND QUEEN MAKE A GRAND ENTRANCE. THEY ARE INDULGING
THEIR NEW STATUS TO THE MAXIMUM, THOUGH MACBETH IS AGITATED.

MACBETH	MACBETH
You each know your position in rank, so be seated!	You know your own degrees; sit down.

THE LORDS TAKE THEIR PLACES ON BOTH SIDES OF
A LONG TABLE ACCORDING TO RANK.

MACBETH ESCORTS LADY MACBETH TO THE HEAD OF THE TABLE.
HE RAISES A GOBLET OF WINE AND GESTURES IT TO BOTH ENDS OF
THE TABLE AS HE MAKES A TOAST.

MACBETH (CONT'D)	MACBETH
From the top to the bottom, I offer a hearty welcome!	At first And last the hearty welcome.

THE LORDS RAISE THEIR CUPS IN A TOAST.

LORDS	LORDS
To the King!	Thanks to your Majesty.

LADY MACBETH SITS. THE LORDS THEN SIT.

MACBETH REMAINS STANDING.

MACBETH	MACBETH
I will mingle with my guests and play the humble host.	Ourself will mingle with society And play the humble host.

MACBETH WALKS THE LENGTH OF THE TABLE.

MACBETH (CONT'D)	MACBETH
Our hostess will remain seated in state, but in good time she will offer her own welcome.	Our hostess keeps her state, but in best time We will require her welcome.

Act III Scene IV. Banqueting Hall. Evening.

LADY MACBETH
Offer it for me, sir,
(*raising her cup*) To all my friends, for
with all my heart they are most welcome.

LADY MACBETH
Pronounce it for me, sir, to all our friends,
For my heart speaks they are welcome.

THE LORDS STAND AND OFFER A TOAST TO THE QUEEN.

MACBETH
(*to Lady Macbeth*) See how they greet you
with heartfelt thanks.

MACBETH
See, they encounter thee with their hearts'
thanks.

MACBETH LOOKS AT THE SEATING.

MACBETH (CONT'D)
The table is evenly filled. I'll sit here
among them.

MACBETH
Both sides are even: here I'll sit i' the midst:

SETON APPEARS AT A DOOR, INDICATING TO MACBETH HE WISHES HIS
ATTENTION.

MACBETH RAISES HIS CUP TO EVERYONE AS HE HEADS FOR SETON.

MACBETH (CONT'D)
(*to all*) Enjoy! Be happy, shortly we'll
drink a measure round the table...

MACBETH
Be large in mirth; anon we'll drink a measure
The table round.

THE LORDS RAISE THEIR CUPS AND CHEER.

AT THE DOOR SETON WHISPERS TO MACBETH, WHO THEN HEADS OUT TO
MEET THE MURDERERS IN A PASSAGE OUTSIDE THE HALL.

MACBETH (CONT'D)
There's blood on your face, man!

MACBETH
There's blood upon thy face.

1ST MURDERER
(*low evil laugh*) That'll be Banquo's then.

MURDERER
'Tis Banquo's then.

MACBETH
(*quietly laughing*) It looks better on you
than in him. Was he '*dispatched*'?

MACBETH
'Tis better thee without than he within.
Is he dispatch'd?

Note: Macbeth almost always uses synonyms for the word 'murder'.

1ST MURDERER
My Lord, I cut his throat for him.

MURDERER
My lord, his throat is cut; that I did for him.

MACBETH
You are number one among cut-throats!
And so is the man who did the same for
Fleance. If that was you too, you would be
above equal.

MACBETH
Thou art the best o' the cut-throats! Yet he's
good
That did the like for Fleance. If thou didst it,
Thou art the nonpareil.

1ˢᵀ MURDERER
Most royal sir... Fleance escaped.

MACBETH
(*angry fit*) I feel my fever returning. I could have been well, smooth as marble, solid as rock, as free and easy as the air about us, but instead I am crushed, cramped, cocooned, bound by my impudent doubts and fears still...
(*calmer*) But Banquo's safely out the way?

1ˢᵀ MURDERER
Yes, my lord, safely in a ditch he lays, with twenty deep trenches in his head, the least of them being fatal.

MACBETH
Thanks for that at least.
(*in thought*) There the grown serpent lies, but the young worm has fled, he has the spirit that in time will breed venom, but for now at least, he has no teeth.
(*to Murderers*) Be gone, we'll speak further tomorrow.

MURDERER
Most royal sir,
Fleance is 'scaped.

MACBETH
Then comes my fit again: I had else been perfect,
Whole as the marble, founded as the rock,
As broad and general as the casing air:
But now I am cabin'd, cribb'd, confined, bound in
To saucy doubts and fears. — But Banquo's safe?

MURDERER
Ay, my good lord. Safe in a ditch he bides,
With twenty trenched gashes on his head;
The least a death to nature.

MACBETH
Thanks for that.
There the grown serpent lies; the worm that's fled
Hath nature that in time will venom breed,
No teeth for the present. Get thee gone.
Tomorrow we'll hear ourselves again.

MACBETH WAVES THE MURDERERS AWAY DISMISSIVELY, AS THEY TURN HE GIVES A NOD TO SETON WHO ACKNOWLEDGES THE SIGN AND SIGNALS THREE GUARDS AT THE END OF THE CORRIDOR.

MACBETH TURNS AND WALKS BACK INTO THE HALL.

AS THE MURDERERS ATTEMPT TO WALK BETWEEN THE GUARDS THEIR EXIT IS BLOCKED. THE MURDERERS LOOK ROUND IN PANIC FOR THE KING, BUT HE HAS LEFT. SETON WALKS UP BEHIND THEM.

MACBETH REJOINS THE FEAST LOOKING A LOT HAPPIER AND RELAXED.

LADY MACBETH
(*loudly*) My royal lord, you are not making your guests welcome. The feast is nothing more than a token gesture if you don't play host and offer good cheer. To just eat we'd best stay home, away from there it is the pomp and ceremony that gives it spice. The company would be dull without it.

LADY MACBETH
My royal lord,
You do not give the cheer. The feast is sold
That is not often vouch'd, while 'tis a-making,
'Tis given with welcome. To feed were best at home;
From thence the sauce to meat is ceremony;
Meeting were bare without it.

Act III Scene IV. Banqueting Hall. Evening.

MACBETH My sweet reminder! Here's to good food and good appetite! A toast to both!	**MACBETH** Sweet remembrancer! Now good digestion wait on appetite, And health on both!

Note: A 'remembrancer' was an aide who reminded the king of his schedule and his duties.

THE LORDS RAISE A CHEERING TOAST IN REPLY.

LORD LENNOX If you please, your Highness, do take your seat.	**LENNOX** May't please your Highness sit.
MACBETH (*ignoring him*) We would have, gathered here under one roof, the entire Scottish nobility, were we graced with the presence of **Banquo**, whom I hope to reprimand for rudeness, rather than pity for some unfortunate event.	**MACBETH** Here had we now our country's honor roof'd, Were the graced person of our Banquo present; Who may I rather challenge for unkindness Than pity for mischance!

Note: Macduff is also absent which makes this speech confusing.

AS MACBETH SAYS THE NAME 'BANQUO', THE BLOODY GHOST OF BANQUO
APPEARS SEATED IN THE SPARE SEAT.

LORD ROSS His absence, sir, is contrary to his promise. Would it please your Highness to grace us with your royal company?	**ROSS** His absence, sir, Lays blame upon his promise. Please't your Highness To grace us with your royal company?
MACBETH The table's full.	**MACBETH** The table's full.
LORD LENNOX Here is an empty place, sir.	**LENNOX** Here is a place reserved, sir.
MACBETH Where?	**MACBETH** Where?
LORD LENNOX Here, my good Lord.	**LENNOX** Here, my good lord.

MACBETH FREEZES AT THE SIGHT OF THE BLOODY FIGURE OF BANQUO
SITTING IN THE CHAIR AS IF A DEAD BODY.

THE CHAIR APPEARS EMPTY TO EVERYONE ELSE. ANOTHER OF HIS VISIONS.

LORD LENNOX (*suddenly worried*) What is it that moves your Highness so?	**LENNOX** What is't that moves your Highness?
MACBETH (*startled, staring*) Which of you did this?	**MACBETH** Which of you have done this?
LORD LENNOX Did what, my Lord?	**LORDS** What, my good lord?

THE LIFELESS BODY OF BANQUO SHOCKS MACBETH BY OPENING ITS EYES.
WITH AN EVIL SMILE IT POINTS DIRECTLY AT MACBETH
AS IF ACCUSING HIM.

MACBETH (*to Ghost*) You cannot say I did it!	**MACBETH** Thou canst not say I did it:

BANQUO'S GHOST LEANS FORWARD SHOWING GAPING HEAD WOUNDS.
IT SHAKES ITS HEAD AND BLOOD SPLASHES OUT OVER THE TABLE.

MACBETH (CONT'D) Don't shake your bloodied locks at me!	**MACBETH** never shake Thy gory locks at me.
LORD ROSS (*standing*) Gentlemen, rise. His Highness is not well.	**ROSS:** Gentlemen, rise; his Highness is not well.

THEY ALL RISE. THE CHAIR STILL APPEARS EMPTY TO EVERYONE ELSE.

LADY MACBETH (*standing*) Sit, dear friends. My Lord is often like this, and has been from youth.	**LADY MACBETH** Sit, worthy friends; my lord is often thus, And hath been from his youth.

THEY ALL SIT NERVOUSLY AGAIN AS LADY MACBETH HEADS FOR MACBETH.

LADY MACBETH (CONT'D) (*to the Lords*) Stay seated, I beg you. The fit is short lived, in a moment he will be well again. If you stare at him you offend him and make him worse. Eat, and ignore him.	**LADY MACBETH** Pray you, keep seat. The fit is momentary; upon a thought He will again be well. If much you note him, You shall offend him and extend his passion: Feed, and regard him not.

LADY MACBETH PUTS HER ARM AROUND MACBETH
AS IF TO CALM HIM, BUT SHE IS FAR FROM HAPPY.

LADY MACBETH (CONT'D) (*to Macbeth only*) Is this the behaviour of a grown man?	**LADY MACBETH** Are you a man?

Act III Scene IV. Banqueting Hall. Evening.

MACBETH POINTS TOWARDS THE GHOSTLY BANQUO.

MACBETH
(*loud for all to hear*) Aye, and a brave one who dares look at that which would appal the Devil himself!

MACBETH
Ay, and a bold one, that dare look on that
Which might appal the devil.

LADY MACBETH
(*to all*) Oh, what nonsense!
(*quietly hissed to Macbeth*) These are the wild imaginings of your fear. Like the airborne dagger you said led you to Duncan.

LADY MACBETH
O proper stuff!
This is the very painting of your fear;
This is the air-drawn dagger which, you said,
Led you to Duncan.

LADY MACBETH GESTURES TO THE LORDS TO
CONTINUE EATING AND DRINKING.

LADY MACBETH (CONT'D)
(*to all*) Oh, these fits and starts, they have no basis in reality...

LADY MACBETH
O, these flaws and starts,
Impostors to true fear,

MACBETH, STILL TRANSFIXED, GESTURES TO THE CHAIR.

LADY MACBETH (CONT'D)
(*hissed to Macbeth*) ...reactions more suited to a woman's ghostly fireside tale, passed down by her grandmother. Shame on you!
(*aloud to Macbeth for all to hear as if making a joke*) Why do you make such faces? You are looking at an empty chair!

LADY MACBETH
would well become
A woman's story at a winter's fire,
Authorized by her grandam. Shame itself!
Why do you make such faces? When all's done,
You look but on a stool.

THOSE GATHERED LAUGH AWKWARDLY AND SYMPATHETICALLY IN
SUPPORT OF LADY MACBETH'S EFFORTS AND EMBARRASSMENT.

MACBETH
I beg you, look there! Look! Can't you see? Now what do you say?

MACBETH
Prithee, see there! Behold! Look! Lo! How say you?

THE GHOST NODS HIS HEAD IN REPLY.

STILL ONLY MACBETH CAN SEE HIM.

MACBETH (CONT'D)

(*to ghost*) What do I care if you can nod your head. Say something, if you can! If cemeteries and graves start sending back those we have buried, we will have to throw their wretched bodies to the vultures in future.

MACBETH

Why, what care I? If thou canst nod, speak too.
If charnel houses and our graves must send
Those that we bury back, our monuments
Shall be the maws of kites.

THE GHOST OF BANQUO FADES AWAY.

LADY MACBETH

Have you lost all control of your senses?

LADY MACBETH

What, quite unmann'd in folly?

MACBETH IS STILL CONFUSED, BUT NOW MORE IN CONTROL.

MACBETH

As sure as I stand here, I saw him.

MACBETH

If I stand here, I saw him.

LADY MACBETH

What nonsense!

LADY MACBETH

Fie, for shame!

LADY MACBETH ANSWERS HIM ALOUD WHILST GESTURING TO THE OTHERS
WHO MAKE A PRETENCE OF IT ALL BEING SILLY HUMOUR, A GAME.

THE NOISE LEVEL RISES AS THE LORDS MAKE A PRETENCE AT JOLLITY.

MACBETH

(*to Lady Macbeth*) Blood has been shed before now, in the unlawful days before peace was brought about – yes, and since then too – murders too terrible to relate. There was a time when a man with his brains dashed out would die and there it would end. But now they rise again with twenty murderous gashes in their heads, and steal our seats. This is more awful than the murder itself.

MACBETH

Blood hath been shed ere now, i' the olden
  time,
Ere humane statute purged the gentle weal;
Ay, and since too, murders have been perform'd
Too terrible for the ear. The time has been,
That, when the brains were out, the man would
  die,
And there an end; but now they rise again,
With twenty mortal murders on their crowns,
And push us from our stools. This is more
  strange
Than such a murder is.

LADY MACBETH

(*condescending*) My Lord. Our noble friends lack your company.

LADY MACBETH

My worthy lord,
Your noble friends do lack you.

MACBETH

I was forgetting.

MACBETH

I do forget.

MACBETH REGAINS HIS COMPOSURE NOW THAT THE GHOST HAS GONE.

MACBETH (CONT'D)

(*to all*) Do not worry about me, my most worthy friends, I have an uncommon condition, which is nothing to those who know me. Come! Health and happiness to all! Give me some wine! Fill me up! Then I'll take my seat. I drink to the joy and happiness of the whole table and to our dear friend **Banquo**, whose company we miss...

MACBETH

Do not muse at me, my most worthy friends.
I have a strange infirmity, which is nothing
To those that know me. Come, love and health
  to all;
Then I'll sit down. Give me some wine, fill full.
I drink to the general joy o' the whole table,
And to our dear friend Banquo, whom we miss.

HE RAISES HIS GLASS TO THE EMPTY SEAT.

MACBETH (CONT'D)

Wish he were here! To all – and to him – we drink! To one and all!

MACBETH

Would he were here! To all and him we thirst,
And all to all.

AS HE TAKES A DRINK, THE GHOST RETURNS TO THE SEAT.

LORDS

To one and all!

LORDS

Our duties and the pledge.

THE GHOST RAISES HIS GLASS TO THE TOAST CAUSING MACBETH TO SPIT OUT HIS MOUTHFUL, SPRAYING NEARBY LORDS.

MACBETH

(*to ghost, madly*) Away! Out of my sight! Back under the earth where you belong with your marrowless bones! Your blood is cold and you see nothing with those eyes you glare at me with!

MACBETH

Avaunt, and quit my sight! Let the earth hide
  thee!
Thy bones are marrowless, thy blood is cold;
Thou hast no speculation in those eyes
Which thou dost glare with.

LADY MACBETH

Think of this, good friends, as just a passing foible. It is nothing more. Only, it rather spoils the fun of the occasion.

LADY MACBETH

Think of this, good peers,
But as a thing of custom. 'Tis no other,
Only it spoils the pleasure of the time.

THE GHOST STANDS UP IN A THREATENING MANNER AND CLIMBS ONTO THE TABLE. IT WALKS DETERMINEDLY TOWARDS MACBETH ALONG THE TABLE, REACHING MACBETH AT THE END OF THE FOLLOWING SPEECH, WHO BY THEN IS IN A FRENZY.

MACBETH
(*to approaching Ghost*) If any *MAN* dares me, I accept the dare! Come at me as a rugged Russian bear, an armoured rhinoceros, or a wild tiger; any shape but your own and my nerves will never falter. Or come alive again and challenge me to a duel in a barren wilderness. If my body trembles, call me a baby girl. Until then, be gone from here vile stalker! False trickery! Be gone!

MACBETH
What man dare, I dare.
Approach thou like the rugged Russian bear,
The arm'd rhinoceros, or the Hyrcan tiger;
Take any shape but that, and my firm nerves
Shall never tremble. Or be alive again,
And dare me to the desert with thy sword.
If trembling I inhabit then, protest me
The baby of a girl. Hence, horrible shadow!
Unreal mockery, hence!

THE GHOST VANISHES AS IT REACHES MACBETH, WHO KEEPS CHANGING
FROM RAGE TO CALM, AS MADMEN OFTEN DO.

MACBETH (CONT'D)
(*calming down*) Why then, now it is gone, I am fine again. Please, everyone stay seated.

MACBETH
Why, so: being gone,
I am a man again. Pray you, sit still.

LADY MACBETH
(*wifely sarcasm*) You have killed the good humour, spoiled the atmosphere with this ridiculous spectacle.

LADY MACBETH
You have displaced the mirth, broke the good meeting,
With most admired disorder.

MACBETH
Can such things come alive, and cast their shadow over us like a summer's cloud without unnerving us? You make me doubt my own strength when I think you can witness such sights and keep the natural blush of your cheeks, while mine are pale with fear.

MACBETH
Can such things be,
And overcome us like a summer's cloud,
Without our special wonder? You make me
  strange
Even to the disposition that I owe,
When now I think you can behold such sights,
And keep the natural ruby of your cheeks
When mine is blanch'd with fear.

LORD ROSS
What sights, my Lord?

ROSS
What sights, my lord?

LADY MACBETH
(*worried he may reveal more than would be safe*) I beg you, don't ask. He gets worse and worse. Questions enrage him. Now, goodnight. Leave without ceremony, all of you, at once.

LADY MACBETH
I pray you, speak not; he grows worse and worse;
Question enrages him. At once, good night:
Stand not upon the order of your going,
But go at once.

THE LORDS ALL RISE.

Act III Scene IV. Banqueting Hall. Evening.

LORD LENNOX

Goodnight, may better health attend his majesty.

LADY MACBETH

(*shooing them out*) A kind goodnight to all!

THE LORDS FILE OUT.

OUTSIDE THE FEASTING HALL THE LORDS GATHER, CONCERNED AT THE BEHAVIOUR OF MACBETH.

GUARDS AND SETON BRING IN A BODY. IT IS COVERED IN A BLOODIED SHROUD. THEY CARRY IT PAST LENNOX WHO WAS IN CONVERSATION WITH ROSS, BUT STOPS TO SILENTLY WATCH IT CARRIED PAST.

LENNOX LIFTS THE COVER TO LOOK AT THE BLOODIED FACE OF BANQUO.

THE LORDS LOOK AT EACH OTHER.

THE INDISTINGUISHABLE DISTANT RAISED VOICE OF LADY MACBETH CAN BE HEARD ADMONISHING MACBETH, CAUSING THE LORDS TO TURN IN ITS DIRECTION.

BACK IN THE FEASTING HALL, MACBETH IS IN HEATED CONVERSATION WITH HIS WIFE.

MACBETH

(*to Lady Macbeth still staring at the empty chair*) It will have blood. That's what they say; "blood will have blood". Gravestones have been known to move and trees to speak. Sages have read the signs, the magpies, rooks and crows have exposed the man with blood on his hands. – Is it still night?

LADY MACBETH

Almost morning, difficult to say which.

MACBETH CALMS ONCE MORE.
AS IF THE PROSPECT OF MORNING IS WELCOME.

MACBETH

What do you think of Macduff ignoring our invitation tonight?

LADY MACBETH

Did you summon him?

LENNOX

Good night, and better health
Attend his Majesty!

LADY MACBETH

A kind good night to all!

MACBETH

It will have blood: they say blood will have blood.
Stones have been known to move and trees to speak;
Augures and understood relations have
By maggot pies and choughs and rooks brought forth
The secret'st man of blood. What is the night?

LADY MACBETH

Almost at odds with morning, which is which.

MACBETH

How say'st thou, that Macduff denies his person
At our great bidding?

LADY MACBETH

Did you send to him, sir?

113

MACBETH BUILDS UP A RAGE AGAIN.

> Note: Earlier, Macbeth said the only person missing was Banquo. Now he mentions Macduff is missing. We know that Macduff also missed Macbeth's coronation (when he was crowned as king).

MACBETH

I hear whispers, I keep a paid servant in all their houses. Tomorrow I'll summon him all right. And before the sun rises I'll visit the weird women. They'll tell me more. I must know the worst, by the worst means.

For my own cause, I'll ensure nothing should
Stand in my way. I have stepped in blood,
I'm in it so deep there's no going back,
So to wade forward is my only tack,
And troublesome plans I have in my scull,
I must act on at once, with no time to mull.

LADY MACBETH

You lack the preservative of all creatures, sleep.

MACBETH

I hear it by the way, but I will send.
There's not a one of them but in his house
I keep a servant fee'd. I will tomorrow,
And betimes I will, to the weird sisters.
More shall they speak; for now I am bent to
  know,
By the worst means, the worst. For mine own good
All causes shall give way. I am in blood
Stepp'd in so far that, should I wade no more,
Returning were as tedious as go o'er.
Strange things I have in head that will to hand,
Which must be acted ere they may be scann'd.

LADY MACBETH

You lack the season of all natures, sleep.

CALM AGAIN. HE IS OBVIOUSLY VERY TIRED, THE PROPHESY OF THE VOICES SAYING MACBETH SHALL SLEEP NO MORE IS TAKING EFFECT.

MACBETH

Come, let us sleep.
My fits and starts are just ignorance
And fear from my lack of experience.
We lack the strength which comes with time.

MACBETH

Come, we'll to sleep. My strange and self-abuse
Is the initiate fear that wants hard use.
We are yet but young in deed.

ACT III SCENE V

A HEATH.

THUNDER AND LIGHTNING.

THREE WITCHES ARE GATHERED. ENTER HECATE.

Note: This scene is usually omitted from performances as it is now believed to have been added some time after Shakespeare wrote the play. It was intended as a musical interlude. It is included here for reference purposes.

WITCH 1

How are you, Hecate? You look angry.

HECATE

Have I not reason, old hags as you are?
You've disobeyed orders. How did you dare
To trade and discuss with Macbeth
Those riddles and affairs of death?

And I, the tutor of your spells
The secret partner in your evils,
Was never called to play my part,
To share the glory of our art?

And, what is worse, what you have done
Was only for a wayward son,
Spiteful and vengeful, who, as others do,
Looks out for himself, and not for you.

So put it right now, get you gone,
And at the Hell of Acheron
Meet me in the morn, where he will be
Coming to know his destiny.

Your cauldrons and your crafts provide,
Your spells and everything beside.
I return up high, this night to spend
Viewing a wretched, fatal end.

FIRST WITCH

Why, how now, Hecate? You look angerly.

HECATE

Have I not reason, beldams as you are,
Saucy and overbold? How did you dare
To trade and traffic with Macbeth
In riddles and affairs of death;

And I, the mistress of your charms,
The close contriver of all harms,
Was never call'd to bear my part,
Or show the glory of our art?

And, which is worse, all you have done
Hath been but for a wayward son,
Spiteful and wrathful: who, as others do,
Loves for his own ends, not for you.

But make amends now. Get you gone,
And at the pit of Acheron
Meet me i' the morning. Thither he
Will come to know his destiny.

Your vessels and your spells provide,
Your charms and every thing beside.
I am for the air; this night I'll spend
Unto a dismal and a fatal end.

Great business must be forged by noon,	Great business must be wrought ere noon:
As on the corner of the moon	Upon the corner of the moon
There hangs a droplet most profound,	There hangs a vaporous drop profound;
I'll catch before it falls to ground.	I'll catch it ere it come to ground.
And that, distilled by magic rites	And that distill'd by magic sleights
Shall raise some supernatural sprites	Shall raise such artificial sprites
That by the power of their illusion	As by the strength of their illusion
Shall lead him awry in his confusion.	Shall draw him on to his confusion.
He shall shun fate, mock death, and bear	He shall spurn fate, scorn death, and bear
Himself above wisdom, grace and fear	His hopes 'bove wisdom, grace, and fear.
And you all know overconfidence	And you all know security
Is mankind's greatest impotence.	Is mortals' chiefest enemy.

AN EERIE CHOIR SINGS.

CHOIR	MUSIC AND SONG
(off) Come away, come away,	*(within)* Come away, come away, etc.
Hecate, Hecate, come away.	
HECATE	HECATE
Listen! I'm called. My little spirit, see,	Hark! I am call'd; my little spirit, see,
(points up) Upon misty cloud, waiting for me.	Sits in a foggy cloud and stays for me.

THE VISION OF HECATE RISES UPWARDS.

WITCH 1	FIRST WITCH
Come, let's hurry. She'll be back again	Come, let's make haste; she'll soon be back
soon.	again.

EXUENT.

> Note: The scene contains music from Thomas Middleton's play The Witch (1615). It is possible Middleton himself inserted the extra scene about the witches and Hecate. Today, most scholars believe all three of the interludes containing the witch, Hecate, were not part of the original play by Shakespeare.

ACT III SCENE VI

THE KING'S PALACE AT FORRES.

LENNOX AND AN UNNAMED SCOTTISH LORD ARE MEETING.

LORD LENNOX	LENNOX
So, what I've been saying aligns with your thinking...	My former speeches have but hit your thoughts,

THE LORD NODS IN AGREEMENT.

LORD LENNOX (CONT'D)	LENNOX
You can draw your own conclusions. All I can say is, there have been strange happenings of late.	Which can interpret farther: only I say Things have been strangely borne.

THE SARCASM IN HIS VOICE INCREASES THROUGHOUT.

LORD LENNOX (CONT'D)	LENNOX
Macbeth sympathized with his "*good compassionate*" ruler, Duncan, – then he was dead. Macbeth's "*good and courageous*" friend Banquo was out walking late, whom you could say – if you accept it – was killed by his own son, because Fleance fled. (*sarcasm*) Obviously a man should not walk so late. Who hasn't thought how monstrous it was for Malcolm and Donalbain to kill their own '*good compassionate*' father? A damnable act! How it angered Macbeth! Didn't he immediately – '*in righteous frenzy*' – tear apart the two useless attendants? Both of them helpless with drink and deep in sleep. Wasn't that a noble act! Oh yes, and righteous too, it would have angered any man alive to hear those men deny their evil deed.	The gracious Duncan Was pitied of Macbeth: marry, he was dead. And the right valiant Banquo walk'd too late, Whom, you may say, if't please you, Fleance kill'd, For Fleance fled. Men must not walk too late. Who cannot want the thought, how monstrous It was for Malcolm and for Donalbain To kill their gracious father? Damned fact! How it did grieve Macbeth! Did he not straight, In pious rage, the two delinquents tear, That were the slaves of drink and thralls of sleep? Was not that nobly done? Ay, and wisely too, For 'twould have anger'd any heart alive To hear the men deny't.

AGAIN THE LORD NODS IN SARCASTIC AGREEMENT.

LORD LENNOX (CONT'D)

So you could say, he has acted in a *'proper'* manner, and I do think that if he had Duncan's sons locked up – which by the grace of God he never will – they'd soon discover the *'proper'* consequences for killing one's own father – and the same goes for Fleance. But all that aside, because of supposed *'rumours'* he's been spreading, and because he failed to present himself at the *'tyrant's'* feast, Macduff has fallen from favour. Do you know where he is at present?

UNNAMED LORD

The son of King Duncan – whose birthright was stolen by this *'tyrant'*, currently resides in the English court of the good King Edward. He is received there with the high esteem and regard of one still in high position. Macduff is headed there now to beg the aid of this most holy King in rousing the Earl of Northumberland and his warlike son Siward to help fight the *'tyrant'*. I pray that with their aid and the backing of God almighty we may again be able to put meat on our table, sleep peacefully at night, hold banquets free from bloody knives, and faithfully serve our *'true'* King, in return for free and fair reward – all things we sorely miss. Macbeth was so angered when he heard the reports he started immediate preparations for war.

LENNOX

So that, I say,
He has borne all things well; and I do think
That, had he Duncan's sons under his key—
As, an't please heaven, he shall not—they should
   find
What 'twere to kill a father; so should Fleance.
But, peace! For from broad words, and 'cause he
   fail'd
His presence at the tyrant's feast, I hear,
Macduff lives in disgrace. Sir, can you tell
Where he bestows himself?

LORD

The son of Duncan,
From whom this tyrant holds the due of birth,
Lives in the English court and is received
Of the most pious Edward with such grace
That the malevolence of fortune nothing
Takes from his high respect. Thither Macduff
Is gone to pray the holy King, upon his aid
To wake Northumberland and warlike Siward;
That by the help of these, with Him above
To ratify the work, we may again
Give to our tables meat, sleep to our nights,
Free from our feasts and banquets bloody
   knives,
Do faithful homage, and receive free honors—
All which we pine for now. And this report
Hath so exasperate the King that he
Prepares for some attempt of war.

> Note: Shakespeare had an unnamed Lord speaking to Lennox. Why he chose a Lord unconnected with the play is unclear. This scene is to move the play forward and explain how the tide is turning against Macbeth.

LORD LENNOX

Did Macbeth not send for Macduff before he left?

LENNOX

Sent he to Macduff?

UNNAMED LORD

Aye, Lennox, he did... but with a firm and final reply of "*Sir, I will not!*" ringing in his ears, the scowling messenger turned his back on Macduff and made the sound of one who says, "*You'll rue the day you gave me this answer to deliver*".

LORD LENNOX

That should be warning enough for Macduff to keep a safe distance. May some swift angelic messenger fly ahead of him to the court of England and shout his message for a swift blessed end to our country's suffering at the hands of this accursed man!

UNNAMED LORD

My prayers go with him.

LORD

He did: and with an absolute "Sir, not I,"
The cloudy messenger turns me his back,
And hums, as who should say, "You'll rue the time
That clogs me with this answer."

LENNOX

And that well might
Advise him to a caution, to hold what distance
His wisdom can provide. Some holy angel
Fly to the court of England and unfold
His message ere he come, that a swift blessing
May soon return to this our suffering country
Under a hand accursed!

LORD

I'll send my prayers with him.

> *Historic Note: King Edward, (Edward the Confessor), son of Æthelred the Unready and Emma of Normandy, was one of the last Anglo-Saxon kings of England, ruling from 1042 to 1066. He was succeeded by Harold who was famously killed at the Battle of Hastings during the Norman Invasion.*
>
> *In the 1050s, Prince Malcolm Canmore was an exile at King Edward's court in England after Macbeth had killed Malcolm's father, King Duncan I, and been awarded the Scottish throne. In 1054 King Edward sent Siward, Earl of Northumbria, to invade Scotland accompanied by Malcolm. By 1058 Malcolm had killed Macbeth in battle and had taken back the Scottish throne. It was a bloody time, as three years later in 1061, Malcolm raided Northumbria with the aim of adding it to his territory.*

End of Act III

ACT IV

THE PROPHESY

TO MACBETH NO HARM SHALL COME
FROM ANY MAN OF WOMAN BORN

ACT IV

ACT IV SCENE I

WITCHES' LAIR AT ACHERON. NIGHT.

THE WITCHES PREPARE A CONCOCTION IN A BUBBLING
CAULDRON WITHIN THEIR LAIR. IT IS HEATED BY A WOOD FIRE.

WITCH 1 STIRS THE CAULDRON.

A STREAKY CAT MEWS THREE TIMES AS IF IN WARNING.

A HEDGEHOG WHINES FOUR TIMES.

THE WITCHES PAUSE AND LOOK AT EACH OTHER.

WITCH 1	FIRST WITCH
Thrice the brindled cat has mewed.	Thrice the brinded cat hath mew'd.
WITCH 2	SECOND WITCH
Thrice plus one, the hedgehog whined.	Thrice and once the hedge-pig whined.

THE DISTANT SHRIEK OF AN OLD HAG IS HEARD CALLING OUT.

WITCH 1	THIRD WITCH
The harpy cries, "It's time, it's time!"	Harpier cries, "'Tis time, 'tis time."

THEY EACH TAKE A BITE FROM A ROOT AND PASS IT ON.

Note: A Harpy is a mythical creature having a woman's head and body with the wings and claws of a giant bird. In Shakespeare's day it also meant a money grabbing, unpleasant woman. It is possibly Witch 3's familiar.

The number three was considered to have mystical powers and is used by the witches frequently as a number or numbers described in multiples of three.

Act IV Scene I. Witches Lair At Acheron. Night.

OUTSIDE THE ROYAL PALACE. NIGHT

MACBETH LEAVES THE CASTLE AND MOUNTS HIS HORSE IN THE DIM LIGHT OF PRE-DAWN, RIDING AWAY FROM THE CASTLE DETERMINEDLY.

LADY MACBETH APPEARS AT A WINDOW AND SEES HIM LEAVE.

ACHERON. WITCHES' LAIR. NIGHT.

WITCH 1 CHANTS AS SHE ADDS POISONS TO THE CAULDRON.

> Note: Each Witch will add a different group of substances.
>
> A toad was laid under a stone for a month (31 days and nights) before venom was extracted while it slept. After that time the venom had reached full strength.

WITCH 1	FIRST WITCH
Round the cauldron, now we go,	*Round about the cauldron go:*
In, the poisoned entrails throw.	*In the poison'd entrails throw.*
Toad that lay beneath cold stone,	*Toad, that under cold stone*
Days and nights count thirty-one,	*Days and nights has thirty-one*
His venom brewed, while sleeping got,	*Swelter'd venom sleeping got,*
Boil this first in our charmed pot	*Boil thou first i' the charmed pot.*

THE WITCHES ALL CHANT AS THE POTION IS STIRRED.

WITCHES	ALL
Double, double, toil and trouble,	*Double, double, toil and trouble;*
Fire burn and cauldron bubble.	*Fire burn and cauldron bubble.*

> Note: "Toil" in this case does not mean labour. In Shakespeare's day a toil was a net or a trap used to catch wildlife, with the double meaning of strife, both made doubly strong (and then doubled again) to catch Macbeth's soul. 'Toil' could be replaced with either 'strife or 'snare' – but it is left here in the original wording as it is so well known.
>
> The second line "Fire burn and cauldron bubble" completes the rhyme, where the Witches are effectively describing to the audience their actions of casting the spell in the first line, and boiling up a potion to make it work in the second. As there were no special effects, scenery, and only limited props, the actors described their actions. Although there was no regard to health and safety back then, it would be very unlikely productions used a real fire on stage.

WITCH 2 ADDS ANIMAL PARTS TO THE POT AND CHANTS HER VERSE.

WITCH 2	SECOND WITCH:
Fillet of a fenland snake,	*Fillet of a fenny snake,*
In the cauldron boil and bake.	*In the cauldron boil and bake;*
Eye of newt and toe of frog,	*Eye of newt and toe of frog,*
Hair of bat and tongue of dog.	*Wool of bat and tongue of dog,*
Adder's tongue and slow-worm's sting,	*Adder's fork and blind-worm's sting,*
Lizard's leg and owlet's wing.	*Lizard's leg and howlet's wing,*
Brew a spell of powerful trouble,	*For a charm of powerful trouble,*
Like a hell-broth, boil and bubble.	*Like a hell-broth boil and bubble.*

THE WITCHES BECOME MORE AFFECTED AND MANIC, AS IF
HALLUCINOGENS ARE TAKING HOLD. THEY ALL CHANT.

WITCHES	ALL
Double, double, toil and trouble,	*Double, double, toil and trouble;*
Fire burn and cauldron bubble.	*Fire burn and cauldron bubble.*

WITCH 3 ADDS EXOTIC INGREDIENTS TO THE POT AND CHANTS.

WITCH 3	THIRD WITCH
Scale of dragon, tooth of boar,	*Scale of dragon, tooth of wolf,*
Powdered witch, guts and gore	*Witch's mummy, maw and gulf*
Of the rav'nous salt-sea shark.	*Of the ravin'd salt-sea shark,*
Root of hemlock dug in the dark,	*Root of hemlock digg'd i' the dark,*
Liver of unholy Jew,	*Liver of blaspheming Jew,*
Gall of goat and sprigs of yew	*Gall of goat and slips of yew*
Gathered in the moon's eclipse,	*Sliver'd in the moon's eclipse,*
Nose of heathen, pagan's lips,	*Nose of Turk and Tartar's lips,*
Finger of birth strangled tot	*Finger of birth-strangled babe*
Fresh delivered by a slut.	*Ditch-deliver'd by a drab,*
Make the mixture thick and hot.	*Make the gruel thick and slab.*
Add to this a tiger's gut,	*Add thereto a tiger's chaudron,*
For this potion in our pot.	*For the ingredients of our cauldron.*

> *Note: Hemlock is a deadly poisonous plant, also referred to by Banquo earlier as 'the insane root'.*
>
> *Jews, muslims, and pagans were considered unholy in a Christian country as they were not baptised.*
>
> *The yew tree is poisonous but popular, as archer's bows were made from it.*
>
> *Turks and Tartars (Mongols), were said to be excessively cruel and violent.*
>
> *A 'drab' was a prostitute. It was rumoured they would give birth to unwanted babies in a ditch and strangle the child to be rid of it.*

WITCHES	ALL
Double, double, toil and trouble,	*Double, double, toil and trouble;*
Fire burn and cauldron bubble.	*Fire burn and cauldron bubble.*

Act IV Scene I. Witches Lair At Acheron. Night.

WITCH 2 POURS IN A DARK RED LIQUID. THE MIXTURE REACTS.

WITCH 2	SECOND WITCH
Cool it with a baboon's blood.	*Cool it with a baboon's blood,*

DIPPING A METAL CUP INTO THE MIXTURE THEY HOLD IT BEFORE THEM.

WITCH 2 (CONT'D)	SECOND WITCH
Then the spell is firm and good.	*Then the charm is firm and good.*

CACKLING THEY DRINK THE MIXTURE AS HECATE (A HEAD WITCH)
PLUS THREE MORE WITCHES ENTER GLEEFULLY.

> *Note: Scholars believe Hecate was not part of Shakespeare's original play.*

HECATE	HECATE
Oh, well done! I praise your pains;	*O, well done! I commend your pains,*
Everyone shall share the gains.	*And everyone shall share i' the gains.*

OUTSIDE THE WITCHES LAIR. JUST BEFORE SUNRISE.

MACBETH RIDES UP TO THE PLACE WHERE HE HAD FIRST
SEEN THE WITCHES BY THE ROCKY OUTCROP.

HE HEARS THE BARELY AUDIBLE SOUND OF FEMALE CHANTING.

HECATE (CONT'D)	HECATE
(distant)	*And now about the cauldron sing,*
And now about the cauldron sing,	*Like elves and fairies in a ring,*
Like elves and fairies in a ring,	*Enchanting all that you put in.*
Enchanting all that you put in.	

A DRUM BEAT SOUNDS IN TIME WITH THE WITCH'S CHANT.

WITCHES	WITCHES
Black spirits, white spirits,	*Black spirits, white spirits,*
Red spirits, and grey	*Red spirits, and grey*
Come out, come out,	*Come out, come out,*
Come out you that may.	*Come out you that may.*

HECATE LEAVES, CACKLING AS SHE GOES.

MACBETH SEES HER LEAVE AND DISMOUNTS
TO INVESTIGATE WHERE SHE CAME FROM.

THE VOICES GET LOUDER AS HE APPROACHES AN ENTRANCE BEHIND THE
ROCK MADE VISIBLE BY THE LIGHT SHOWING THROUGH A CRACK AROUND
A ROUGH DOOR WHICH BARS HIS WAY.

Note: **Spoiler alert** The prophecies Macbeth is about to hear from the Witches will make him fearless and out of control. Later we will see the fear return when the prophecies true meaning becomes apparent to him.

INSIDE THE WITCHES' LAIR.

WITCHES (CONT'D)
And now around the cauldron sing
Like elves and fairies in a ring
Enchanting all that we put in.
Around, around, about, about,
Let evil in, keep all good out...

THERE IS MUSIC AND A SONG
"BLACK SPIRITS"

THE WITCHES SUDDENLY STOP THEIR CHANTING AROUND THE CAULDRON
AS IF THEY HAD SENSED OR HEARD SOMETHING.

WITCH 2
By the tingling in my thumbs
Something wicked this way comes.

SECOND WITCH
By the pricking of my thumbs,
Something wicked this way comes:

A KNOCKING FROM THE ROUGH WOODEN DOOR.

WITCH 2 (CONT'D)
Open the locks,
Whoever knocks!

SECOND WITCH
Open, locks,
Whoever knocks!

THE DOOR OPENS. MACBETH ENTERS THE
LOW DOORWAY, HEAD STOOPED.

MACBETH
What are you up to you secret, dark, satanic hags?

MACBETH
How now, you secret, black, and midnight hags?
What is't you do?

WITCH 1
A deed which has no name.

ALL
A deed without a name.

Witch 1 steps up to Macbeth. She places the root the Witches had bitten earlier into her mouth and bites a chunk off, then places it in Macbeth's mouth as if he is to do the same.

Macbeth bites a chunk off the root and chews, reacting to the horrible taste. He recovers and chews with vigour, showing he'd do anything in his quest for power.

MACBETH	MACBETH
I order that by use of the art you practise – however you came by it – you answer me...	I conjure you, by that which you profess, Howe'er you come to know it, answer me:

The Witches stop and all look at each other with glee.

A wind starts howling, it increases in strength throughout Macbeth's speech. The Witches' clothing blows in the wind from the open door.

MACBETH (CONT'D)	MACBETH
Even if the winds you unleash batter our churches, or dash and swallow ships with foaming waves, or flatten the new grown corn and fell the trees...	Though you untie the winds and let them fight Against the churches, though the yeasty waves Confound and swallow navigation up, Though bladed corn be lodged and trees blown down,

Note: Again, a reference to witches affecting ships, for the benefit of King James.

Witch 2 guides Macbeth to the cauldron where Witch 3 gives him a drink of the murky contents from a ladle as Macbeth continues talking.

MACBETH (CONT'D)	MACBETH
....Even if those winds bring castles crashing down about their owner's heads, or palaces and pyramids crumbling to their foundations. Even if the seeds of nature's creation tumble together to consume and destroy themselves, even then you will answer all that I ask you.	Though castles topple on their warders' heads, Though palaces and pyramids do slope Their heads to their foundations, though the treasure Of nature's germens tumble all together Even till destruction sicken, answer me To what I ask you.

The wind reaches a crescendo and the door blows shut with a resounding bang.

At this point, the room is swirling for Macbeth and he is struggling to focus.

WITCH 1	FIRST WITCH
Ask.	Speak.
WITCH 2	**SECOND WITCH**
Demand.	Demand.
WITCH 3	**THIRD WITCH**
We will answer.	We'll answer.

THE WITCHES FORCE MACBETH'S HEAD TO LOOK INTO THE CAULDRON. HE IS GLASSY EYED AND TO HIM THE BUBBLING CONTENTS ARE DISTORTED, AS IF HALLUCINATIONS HAVE BEGUN.

HE SEES HIS OWN FACE DISTORTED IN THE REFLECTION. IT LOOKS UGLY AND HIDEOUS. THE WITCHES' FACES, BY CONTRAST, NOW APPEAR ATTRACTIVE TO MACBETH, CONFUSING HIM. EVERYTHING SEEMS OPPOSITE TO HOW IT WAS BEFORE.

WITCH 1	FIRST WITCH
Say if you'd rather hear it from our mouths or from those who rule us.	Say, if thou'dst rather hear it from our mouths, or from our masters?
MACBETH	**MACBETH**
Call them. Let me see them.	Call 'em, let me see 'em.
WITCH 1	**FIRST WITCH**
Pour in sow's blood that has eaten	*Pour in sow's blood that hath eaten*
Her nine young, and grease that's beaten	*Her nine farrow; grease that's sweaten*
From the wooden gibbet's frame;	*From the murderer's gibbet throw*
Throw it now into the flame...	*Into the flame.*

THEY ADD IT TO THE MIXTURE. THE LIQUID REACTS AND THE FIRE FLARES UP IN VIVID FLAME AND COLOUR.

Note: *Bodies left hanging in the gibbet for days in sunshine would drip fat (grease) onto the wooden gallows frame which would then congeal. The last person to be gibbeted in England was in 1832.*

Sows (female pigs) that ate their young were considered evil and slaughtered.

WITCHES	ALL
Come from high hell or from low	*Come, high or low;*
Yourself in likeness to us show!	*Thyself and office deftly show!*

A SOUND LIKE NO OTHER HEARD BY MORTAL MAN RINGS OUT AS THE MIXTURE BUBBLES FURIOUSLY AND A HUMAN HEAD WEARING ARMOUR APPEARS, RISING UP THROUGH THE SURFACE OF THE LIQUID.

THE FACE BREAKS THE SURFACE. IT LOOKS LIKE THE FACE OF MACBETH.

Note: ***Spoiler Alert** The dismembered head prophesying Macbeth's own beheading and the perpetrator of it.*

MACBETH	**MACBETH**
Tell me, you unknown power...	Tell me, thou unknown power,–
WITCH 1	**FIRST WITCH**
(*interrupting*) He knows your thoughts. Hear his words but say nothing.	He knows thy thought: Hear his speech, but say thou nought.

AS THE HEAD SPEAKS, RED LIQUID SPILLS FROM ITS MOUTH.

APPARITION 1	**FIRST APPARITION**
Macbeth! Macbeth! Macbeth! Beware Macduff *Beware the Lord of Fife. Dismiss me. Enough!*	*Macbeth! Macbeth! Macbeth! Beware Macduff;* *Beware the Thane of Fife. Dismiss me. Enough.*

THE HEAD SINKS BELOW THE BUBBLING SURFACE.

MACBETH	**MACBETH**
Whatever you are, I thank you for your good warning. You have confirmed my fears. But one more question...	Whate'er thou art, for thy good caution, thanks; Thou hast harp'd my fear aright. But one word more–
WITCH 1	**FIRST WITCH**
He will not be ordered. Here's another, more powerful than the first.	He will not be commanded. Here's another, More potent than the first.

WITCH 1 POURS SOMETHING HORRIBLE INTO THE POT. IT REACTS.
MACBETH IS GIVEN ANOTHER LADLE FULL OF POTION TO DRINK.

THUNDER ROARS.

A BLOODIED CHILD'S HEAD APPEARS FROM THE LIQUID.

APPARITION 2	**SECOND APPARITION**
(*child*) Macbeth! Macbeth! Macbeth!	Macbeth! Macbeth! Macbeth!
MACBETH	**MACBETH**
(*now appearing drugged*) Have I three ears? I hear you!	Had I three ears, I'd hear thee.
APPARITION 2	**SECOND APPARITION**
Be brutal, bold, steadfast and strong, *Laugh and mock the power of man.* *For to Macbeth no harm shall come* *From any man of woman born.*	*Be bloody, bold, and resolute; laugh to scorn* *The power of man, for none of woman born* *Shall harm Macbeth.*

APPARITION 2 SLOWLY SINKS BENEATH THE LIQUID.

MACBETH PONDERS THE WORDS FOR A MOMENT.

Note: Another part of the prophesy. A man not of woman born. Macbeth will learn the true meaning behind this statement later.

MACBETH

(*realisation*) Then live on, Macduff! I need not fear you. Though to be doubly sure fate is on my side you shall <u>not</u> live on. That will calm my weak-hearted fears, and I can sleep again through even the wildest storm.

MACBETH

Then live, Macduff. What need I fear of thee? But yet I'll make assurance double sure, And take a bond of fate: thou shalt not live, That I may tell pale-hearted fear it lies, And sleep in spite of thunder.

> Note: Again, Macbeth refers to lack of sleep, which is slowly driving him mad.

APPARITION 3 APPEARS, A CHILD WITH A CROWN UPON ITS HEAD AND HOLDING A TREE BRANCH ABOVE THE SURFACE OF THE LIQUID.

MACBETH (CONT'D)

What is this that rises in the likeness of a King and wearing the round symbol of sovereignty upon its infant brow?

MACBETH

What is this, That rises like the issue of a king, And wears upon his baby brow the round And top of sovereignty?

> Note: Another prophesy, this one hinting at the child of Banquo to be king after Birnam Wood (symbolised by the tree branch) comes to Dunsinane.

WITCH 1

Listen, but speak not to it.

ALL

Listen, but speak not to't.

APPARITION 3

(*a male child*)
Be lion hearted, proud, and have no care
Who scorns, nor worry where conspirers are:
For Macbeth shall not defeated be 'till
Birnam Wood comes to Dunsinane Hill,
To stand before him...

THIRD APPARITION

Be lion-mettled, proud, and take no care
Who chafes, who frets, or where conspirers are:
Macbeth shall never vanquish'd be until
Great Birnam Wood to high Dunsinane Hill
Shall come against him.

THE APPARITION SINKS BACK INTO THE LIQUID.

MACBETH'S VISION IS SWIRLING AND BLURRED, HE IS NOW FULLY UNDER THE INFLUENCE OF THE HALLUCINOGENS.

MACBETH

That can never be. Who can command a forest, or order a tree to uproot its earthbound bond? This bodes well! Good! Until Birnam Wood rises up against me, no rebellion shall. – Then our Royal Macbeth shall live the full lease of nature, drawing his breath to the end of his natural life. Yet my heart yearns to know one more thing...

MACBETH

That will never be. Who can impress the forest, bid the tree Unfix his earth-bound root? Sweet bodements, good! Rebellion's head, rise never, till the Wood Of Birnam rise, and our high-placed Macbeth Shall live the lease of nature, pay his breath To time and mortal custom. Yet my heart Throbs to know one thing...

Act IV Scene I. Witches Lair At Acheron. Night.

> Note: Originally the line was printed 'Rebellion's dead, rise never, till the Wood of Birnam rise', (perhaps the earliest mention of a zombie apocalypse) but most editions consider this an error and use 'Rebellion's head'.

MACBETH LOOKS AT THE WITCHES AROUND THE CAULDRON, THEIR FACES AND BODIES NOW APPEAR BEAUTIFUL TO HIM.

MACBETH (CONT'D)
(*to witches*) Tell me, if your art can tell me such things, will Banquo's offspring ever reign in this Kingdom?

WITCH 1
Seek to know no more.

MACBETH
(*angry, mix of drugs and insanity*) I will be answered! May an eternal curse be placed upon you if you refuse me! Let me know now!

MACBETH
tell me, if your art
Can tell so much, shall Banquo's issue ever
Reign in this kingdom?

ALL
Seek to know no more.

MACBETH
I will be satisfied! Deny me this,
And an eternal curse fall on you! Let me know:

A CACOPHONY OF SOUND AS THE CAULDRON SINKS INTO THE GROUND.

> Note: Original stage direction says 'Hautboys' (ancient oboes). Music was played for dramatic effect. Sound effects were simple or non existent.

MACBETH (CONT'D)
Why does the cauldron sink into the ground? ... What is that noise?

WITCH 1
Show!

WITCH 2
Show!

WITCH 3
Show!

WITCHES
Show his eyes, burden his heart;
Come like shadows, then depart.

MACBETH
Why sinks that cauldron? and what noise is this?

FIRST WITCH
Show!

SECOND WITCH
Show!

THIRD WITCH
Show!

ALL
Show his eyes, and grieve his heart;
Come like shadows, so depart!

RISING FROM THE HOLE WHERE THE POT SANK IS A YOUNG BANQUO WEARING A CROWN. HE WALKS AWAY, VANISHING THROUGH THE WALL.

MACBETH
You look too like the ghost of Banquo. Leave! Your crown burns my eyes...

MACBETH
Thou are too like the spirit of Banquo. Down!
Thy crown does sear mine eyeballs.

A SECOND BANQUO DESCENDANT RISES FROM THE POT,
REPEATING THE EXACT SAME ACTIONS AS THE ONE BEFORE.

MACBETH (CONT'D)	MACBETH
And your hair, your other golden crown, is like the first.	And thy hair, Thou other gold-bound brow, is like the first.

AS THE SECOND ONE WALKS OFF A THIRD APPEARS.

MACBETH (CONT'D)	MACBETH
And a third like the others. Filthy hags! Why do you show me this?	A third is like the former. Filthy hags! Why do you show me this?

THE THIRD WALKS OFF AS A FOURTH APPEARS.

MACBETH (CONT'D)	MACBETH
A fourth? It hurts my eyes!	A fourth! Start, eyes!

THE FOURTH WALKS OFF AS A FIFTH APPEARS.

MACBETH (CONT'D)	MACBETH
What? Will the line stretch out to the end of time?	What, will the line stretch out to the crack of doom?

THE FIFTH WALKS OFF AS A SIXTH APPEARS.

MACBETH (CONT'D)	MACBETH
Yet another?	Another yet!

THE SIXTH WALKS OFF AS A SEVENTH APPEARS.

MACBETH (CONT'D)	MACBETH
A seventh! Show me no more!	A seventh! I'll see no more:

THE SEVENTH WALKS OFF AND AN EIGHTH APPEARS HOLDING A MIRROR
WHICH SHOWS A MIRROR EFFECT OF A LINE OF IDENTICAL FIGURES EXCEPT
FOR EACH WEARING OR CARRYING DIFFERENT SYMBOLS.

MACBETH (CONT'D)	MACBETH
And still an eighth appears, holding a mirror showing many more. And some I see carrying the emblems of a united England, Scotland and Ireland. Horrible sight!	And yet the eighth appears, who bears a glass Which shows me many more; and some I see That twofold balls and treble sceptres carry: Horrible sight!

Act IV Scene I. Witches Lair At Acheron. Night.

THE BLOODIED FACE OF THE GHOST OF BANQUO APPEARS IN THE
MIRROR SMIRKING, AND POINTS DOWN THE LINE OF KINGS SMUGLY.

MACBETH (CONT'D)	MACBETH
Now I see it's true, the blood-spattered Banquo smiles at me and points to the kings as his descendants.	Now I see 'tis true; For the blood-bolter'd Banquo smiles upon me, And points at them for his.

Note: The eight kings of the Scottish house of Stuart, from Robert II to James VI.
According to Holinshed, (whose book Shakespeare based his historical
knowledge on) the lineage of James, King of England and Scotland, can be traced
back to Banquo. This is historically incorrect but believed by King James.

IMPORTANT – The following line by Macbeth and the song and dance of the
Witches that follows it was added later by another hand. It is in a different style
and meter to Shakespeare. Macbeth having just stated, "Now I see it's true",
follows here with the confusing line," What, is this so?" We can skip forward to
the next morning and miss nothing.

MACBETH (CONT'D)	MACBETH
(to Witches) What! Will this happen?	What, is this so?

THE ATTRACTIVE VERSIONS OF THE WITCHES (IN MACBETH'S ALTERED
MIND) START DANCING AND SINGING IN MACBETH'S BLURRED VISION.

WITCH 1	FIRST WITCH
Yes, all this will happen. But why	Ay, sir, all this is so. But why
Stands Macbeth so amazedly?	Stands Macbeth thus amazedly?
Come sisters, cheer away his frights,	Come, sisters, cheer we up his sprites,
And show the best of our delights -	And show the best of our delights.
I'll cast a spell to play a sound,	I'll charm the air to give a sound,
While you perform and dance around,	While you perform your antic round,
So this great King may kindly say	That this great King may kindly say
Our duties have been duly paid.	Our duties did his welcome pay.

MACBETH CANNOT FOCUS, HE SLUMPS IN A STUPOR IN THE CORNER.

A Heath Next To A Rocky Outcrop. Dawn.

Lennox, and others out riding early, see Macbeth's horse grazing by the rocky outcrop. They ride over to investigate. Lennox dismounts.

He checks Macbeth's horse. It is still saddled to ride. He lifts a brass and sees the royal emblem.

He looks towards the rocky outcrop, seeing footprints in the earth leading to it but is then distracted by a couple of horses galloping towards him.

Inside The Witches' Lair. Dawn.

Macbeth is slumped against a wall, exhausted.

The sound of horses outside rouses Macbeth. He looks around confused. The fire is now embers. This is the only trace of the previous night's activities. He has no idea how long he has been sitting there. It seemed only moments since the Witches left.

MACBETH	MACBETH
(*looking around*) Where are they? Have they gone? May this evil hour stand forever marked as cursed in the calendar.	Where are they? Gone! Let this pernicious hour Stand aye accursed in the calendar!

The door starts opening. Macbeth puts a hand to his sword.

MACBETH (CONT'D)	MACBETH
(*calling out*) Who's out there!	Come in, without there!

Lennox enters.

LORD LENNOX	LENNOX
I am at your service, your Highness.	What's your Grace's will?
MACBETH	MACBETH
Lennox! Did you see the weird women?	Saw you the weird sisters?
LORD LENNOX	LENNOX
(*concerned at Macbeth's sanity*) No, my Lord?	No, my lord.

134

MACBETH
They did not pass you?

MACBETH
Came they not by you?

LORD LENNOX
Indeed not, my Lord.

LENNOX
No indeed, my lord.

MACBETH
May the air they ride on be damned, and all those who believe them! I heard horses outside, who rode by?

MACBETH
Infected be the air whereon they ride, And damn'd all those that trust them! I did hear The galloping of horse. Who was't came by?

Note: Macbeth is damning himself as he believes what they showed him.

LORD LENNOX
Two or three men, my Lord, bringing you news that Macduff has fled to England.

LENNOX
'Tis two or three, my lord, that bring you word Macduff is fled to England.

MACBETH
Fled to England?

MACBETH
Fled to England?

LORD LENNOX
Aye, my Lord.

LENNOX
Ay, my good lord.

Note: Macbeth now speaks his fifth soliloquy.

MACBETH
(*to self*) Time, you anticipate my direst deeds. Only if we act swiftly do our plans succeed. From now on, the moment I have a thought shall be the moment I act. And now, to practise what I preach, my thought will be done: I'll storm Macduff's castle, seize Fife, and show the edge of my sword to his wife and children, and any other unfortunate souls of his bloodline.
The deed'll be done, no boasting like fools,
Before my purpose wanes and cools.
And bring an end to these visions!
(*aloud to Lennox*) Where are these messengers? Take me to them!

MACBETH
(*aside*) Time, thou anticipatest my dread exploits.
The flighty purpose never is o'ertook
Unless the deed go with it. From this moment
The very firstlings of my heart shall be
The firstlings of my hand. And even now,
To crown my thoughts with acts, be it thought and
  done:
The castle of Macduff I will surprise,
Seize upon Fife; give to the edge o' the sword
His wife, his babes, and all unfortunate souls
That trace him in his line. No boasting like a fool;
This deed I'll do before this purpose cool.
But no more sights! –Where are these gentlemen?
Come, bring me where they are.

LENNOX TURNS AND EXITS THE LAIR FOLLOWED BY MACBETH.

ACT IV SCENE II

MACDUFF'S CASTLE, FIFE.

> *Note: This scene is not for the faint hearted. It was often excluded from later productions due to it's horrific content and was considered unsuitable for children, though not in Shakespeare's day, where children were taken to watch public executions.*
>
> *Queen Elizabeth signed a decree permitting young boys to be 'stolen' by theatre companies and forced to perform. They were often kidnapped on their way home from school and whipped if they didn't perform. Distraught parents could do nothing, and in one famous case a father tried to steal back his 13 year old son, Thomas Clifton, but was physically restrained. Troops of performing children were popular among predominantly male audiences, with dubious morals. Shakespeare deplored this use of children and spoke out against it, most notably in Hamlet. Even Marlowe, a contemporary playwright, included one very dubious scene involving a boy in 'Dido'.*

LADY MACDUFF, HER SON, DAUGHTER, AND HER
COUSIN, ROSS, ARE TALKING FEARFULLY.

LADY MACDUFF
What had my husband done to make him flee the country, Ross?

LORD ROSS
You must have patience, madam.

LADY MACDUFF
Well, he had none. Fleeing was madness. We've done nothing, and now his fear makes us seem traitors.

LORD ROSS
Lord Macduff may have fled for good reason, rather than fear.

LADY MACDUFF
Good reason! To leave his wife? To leave his children, his possessions and his titles in the very place he fled from? He does not love us. He has no paternal feelings. Even the puny wren, the smallest of birds, will fight to protect her young from an attacking owl. This is all fear, nothing to do with love, and little to do with reason where the flight runs against all common sense.

LADY MACDUFF
What had he done, to make him fly the land?

ROSS
You must have patience, madam.

LADY MACDUFF
He had none;
His flight was madness. When our actions do not,
Our fears do make us traitors.

ROSS
You know not
Whether it was his wisdom or his fear.

LADY MACDUFF
Wisdom? To leave his wife, to leave his babes,
His mansion, and his titles, in a place
From whence himself does fly? He loves us not;
He wants the natural touch: for the poor wren,
The most diminutive of birds, will fight,
Her young ones in her nest, against the owl.
All is the fear and nothing is the love;
As little is the wisdom, where the flight
So runs against all reason.

Act IV Scene II. Macduff's Castle. Fife.

LORD ROSS	ROSS
My dearest cousin, I beg you, see reason. Your husband is honourable, wise, and in the best position to judge the current situation. I dare not say more, but times are cruel when we are branded traitors and know not who to trust. All we hear are fearful rumours, but don't know which ones to fear. We drift on a wild and violent sea at the mercy of the tide.	My dearest coz, I pray you, school yourself. But for your husband, He is noble, wise, judicious, and best knows The fits o' the season. I dare not speak much further; But cruel are the times, when we are traitors And do not know ourselves; when we hold rumor From what we fear, yet know not what we fear, But float upon a wild and violent sea Each way and move.

> Note: 'Ourselves' - each other. You can trust no one when Macbeth has spies in every household.

LADY MACDUFF PULLS HER CHILDREN TO HER, DRESSING THEM
NERVOUSLY AS IF PREPARING TO LEAVE AS HE SPEAKS.

LORD ROSS (CONT'D)	ROSS
I must leave. I'll return as soon as I can. Times are at their worst, they have to end soon, and hopefully rise again to how they used to be.	I take my leave of you; Shall not be long but I'll be here again. Things at the worst will cease, or else climb upward To what they were before.

HE KISSES HER FAREWELL.

> Note: Some publications suggest Ross's next line is to the boy, though the wording is strange to be directed at a young boy.

LORD ROSS (CONT'D)	ROSS
My beautiful cousin, may God bless and care for you!	My pretty cousin, Blessing upon you!
LADY MACDUFF	**LADY MACDUFF**
My son here has a father, yet he is fatherless.	Father'd he is, and yet he's fatherless.

TEARS FORM IN THE EYES OF LORD ROSS.

LORD ROSS	ROSS
(*trying to hold back his emotion*) I am such a fool. If I stay any longer I would disgrace myself and embarrass you with my tears. I must leave at once.	I am so much a fool, should I stay longer, It would be my disgrace and your discomfort. I take my leave at once.

137

ROSS LEAVES. LADY MACDUFF DRESSES THE CHILDREN.

LADY MACDUFF
My poor child, your father's dead. What will you do now? How will you live?

SON
Like a bird, mother.

LADY MACDUFF
What, on worms and flies?

SON
With whatever I can find, I mean, just as birds do.

LADY MACDUFF
My poor sparrow! But wouldn't you be afraid of traps set to catch birds?

> Note: 'Lime' - birdlime. A sticky substance, often made by boiling holly bark and mixing it with nut oil, it was smeared on tree branches to trap small birds.
>
> A 'gin' trap was used to snare small animals and birds. A 'pitfall' was a covered trap the prey would fall into, now used to mean hidden or unexpected danger.

SON
Why should I be, mother? They are not set for 'poor sparrows'. And anyway my father's not dead, as you keep saying.

LADY MACDUFF
Yes, he is dead. What will you do for a father?

SON
No, what will you do for a husband?

LADY MACDUFF
Oh, I can buy twenty of them at any market.

SON
Twenty? Then you are buying them to sell again.

LADY MACDUFF
You make little sense, but you have wit for one so young.

SON
Was my father a traitor, mother?

LADY MACDUFF
Aye, he was.

LADY MACDUFF
Sirrah, your father's dead.
And what will you do now? How will you live?

SON
As birds do, Mother.

LADY MACDUFF
What, with worms and flies?

SON
With what I get, I mean; and so do they.

LADY MACDUFF
Poor bird! Thou'ldst never fear the net nor lime,
The pitfall nor the gin.

SON
Why should I, Mother? Poor birds they are not set for.
My father is not dead, for all your saying.

LADY MACDUFF
Yes, he is dead. How wilt thou do for a father?

SON
Nay, how will you do for a husband?

LADY MACDUFF
Why, I can buy me twenty at any market.

SON
Then you'll buy 'em to sell again.

LADY MACDUFF
Thou speak'st with all thy wit, and yet, i' faith,
With wit enough for thee.

SON
Was my father a traitor, Mother?

LADY MACDUFF
Ay, that he was.

Modern	Original
SON What is a traitor?	**SON** What is a traitor?
LADY MACDUFF Someone who swears a solemn vow, then breaks it by lying.	**LADY MACDUFF** Why, one that swears and lies.
SON Is everyone who does so a traitor?	**SON** And be all traitors that do so?
LADY MACDUFF Everyone who does so is a traitor and must be hanged.	**LADY MACDUFF** Everyone that does so is a traitor and must be hanged.
SON Everyone must be hanged who swears and lies?	**SON** And must they all be hanged that swear and lie?
LADY MACDUFF Every one of them.	**LADY MACDUFF** Every one.
SON Who hangs them?	**SON** Who must hang them?
LADY MACDUFF Well, the honest men.	**LADY MACDUFF** Why, the honest men.
SON Then the liars and swearers are fools. There are enough liars and swearers to beat the honest men and hang them instead.	**SON** Then the liars and swearers are fools; for there are liars and swearers enough to beat the honest men and hang up them.
LADY MACDUFF (*laughing*) Heaven help you, poor little monkey!	**LADY MACDUFF** Now, God help thee, poor monkey!

Note: The previous exchange was wordplay on several fronts.

First, Macduff swore a vow of marriage to stand by his wife, and he broke that vow.

Secondly, he swore allegiance to his King, Macbeth, and broke that vow.

Thirdly, another reference to the Gunpowder Plot – the priest swearing on the bible and then lying on oath in court, and how Guy Fawkes should have been hanged (and drawn and quartered) but instead he jumped to his death.

Finally, jokey banter about hanging the honest men who didn't do their job properly – probably made for the King's benefit (who was in the audience). Shakespeare repeats the 'swear/lie' combination four times ensuring the king understood. Shakespeare adds the line that all men who do so should be hanged as traitors, a veiled sycophantic line for King James' benefit.

| **LADY MACDUFF (CONT'D)**
 (*sad again*) But what will you do for a father? | **LADY MACDUFF**
 But how wilt thou do for a father? |

SON

If he were dead, you'd be weeping for him. As you are not, I'll take it as a good sign that I'll soon have a new father.

LADY MACDUFF

Poor thing, my, how you prattle on!

SON

If he were dead, you'd weep for him: if you would not, it were a good sign that I should quickly have a new father.

LADY MACDUFF

Poor prattler, how thou talk'st!

A MESSENGER RUSHES IN.
LADY MACDUFF EXCLAIMS IN SHOCKED SURPRISE, FEARFULLY
GRABBING THE CHILDREN TO HER, NOT RECOGNISING THE MAN.

MESSENGER

(*urgent, fearful*) God bless you, good lady. Although I'm not known to you, I am familiar with your situation, and I'm fearful of the danger heading your way. If you'll take a humble man's advice, do not stay here. Leave at once with your little ones! It may seem cruel of me, frightening you in this way, but believe me, far greater cruelty approaches. May Heaven preserve you, madam! I daren't stay any longer.

MESSENGER

Bless you, fair dame! I am not to you known,
Though, in your state of honor I am perfect.
I doubt some danger does approach you nearly.
If you will take a homely man's advice,
Be not found here; hence, with your little ones.
To fright you thus, methinks I am too savage;
To do worse to you were fell cruelty,
Which is too nigh your person. Heaven preserve you!
I dare abide no longer.

THE MESSENGER EXITS CLOSING THE DOOR BEHIND HIM.
LADY MACDUFF HOLDS HER CHILDREN TO HER NERVOUSLY.

LADY MACDUFF

Where should I run? I've done no wrong.

LADY MACDUFF

Whither should I fly?
I have done no harm.

SOUNDS OF DISTANT SMASHING AND DESTRUCTION ACCOMPANIED BY
MALE SHOUTS AND FEMALE SCREAMS.

LADY MACDUFF RUNS AND LOCKS THE DOOR, TALKING WHILE LOOKING
AROUND AS IF TRYING TO FIND SOME WAY OUT OR A HIDING PLACE.

LADY MACDUFF (CONT'D)

But I was forgetting, I'm in a world where doing wrong is often commendable, while doing good can be dangerous and foolish. Why then, do I put up that feeble excuse that I have done nothing wrong?

LADY MACDUFF

But I remember now
I am in this earthly world, where to do harm
Is often laudable, to do good sometime
Accounted dangerous folly. Why then, alas,
Do I put up that womanly defense,
To say I have done no harm?

Note: In a male dominated time, 'womanly' signified weak and feeble.

140

INVADERS HAVE STORMED THE CASTLE, ATTACKING UNARMED MALE
SERVANTS, SMASHING ALL IN THEIR PATH. WOMEN ARE TAKEN BY FORCE.

LADY MACDUFF LISTENS IN HORROR AS BARBARIC SOUNDS OF VIOLENCE,
SMASHING, SHOUTING AND SCREAMS COME CLOSER.

THE DOOR HANDLE MOVES AS SOMEONE TRIES TO ENTER THE ROOM.
SHE PICKS UP HER TWO CHILDREN AND COWERS IN A CORNER.

THE DOOR BEHIND HER IS SMASHED WITH FORCE. THE DOOR GIVES AND
THE BARBARIC ATTACKERS BURST THROUGH THE DOOR. SNEERING WITH
GLEE, LED BY SETON. HE HAS FOUND WHAT HE WAS LOOKING FOR.

LADY MACDUFF (CONT'D)	LADY MACDUFF
Who are these people?	What are these faces?
SETON	FIRST MURDERER
Where's your husband?	Where is your husband?
LADY MACDUFF	LADY MACDUFF
Not, I hope, in a place so unholy that you'd be able to find him.	I hope, in no place so unsanctified Where such as thou mayst find him.
SETON	FIRST MURDERER
He's a traitor.	He's a traitor.
SON	SON
You lie, you long haired bastard!	Thou liest, thou shag-ear'd villain!

THE SON BREAKS FROM HIS MOTHER AND RUNS AT THE INVADER.

SETON	FIRST MURDERER
What was that, shrimp?	What, you egg!

THE SON PUMMELS ON THE INVADER'S CHEST INEFFECTUALLY
THEN STOPS AND LOOKS DOWN. SETON'S DAGGER IS BLOODY.

SETON (CONT'D)	FIRST MURDERER
Spawn of treachery!	Young fry of treachery!

THE SON PUTS HIS HAND TO HIS STOMACH. BLOOD POURS THROUGH HIS
FINGERS. IN HORRIFIED REALISATION HE CRIES OUT AS HE COLLAPSES TO
HIS KNEES CLUTCHING HIS STOMACH...

SON	SON
Mother! He's killed me.	He has kill'd me, Mother.

THE INVADER SMILES EVILY AT THE MOTHER AND HEADS TO HER.

SON (CONT'D)	SON
Run away, I beg you!	Run away, I pray you!

THE SON FALLS DOWN WITH HIS ARM REACHING OUT FOR HIS MOTHER, BEFORE DYING.

LADY MACDUFF PICKS UP THE POKER FROM THE FIRE TO DEFEND HERSELF AND HER YOUNG DAUGHTER IN HER ARMS. THE CHILD IS CRYING FEARFULLY.

LADY MACDUFF	LADY MACDUFF
Murderer!	Murder!

SHE RUNS AT HIM, SWINGING THE POKER WILDLY. HIS STRONG HAND CATCHES HER WRIST. SMILING HE SQUEEZES AND TWISTS TILL THE POKER FALLS FROM HER HAND.

HE LOOKS AT THE CHILD IN HER ARMS AND THEN AT THE MOTHER.

LADY MACDUFF SCREAMS IN HORROR AT THE REALISATION OF WHAT IS TO COME.

ACT IV SCENE III

THE ENGLISH KING'S PALACE GROUNDS

PRINCE MALCOLM, EXILED TRUE HEIR TO THE SCOTTISH THRONE, IS TALKING WITH MACDUFF WHILE THEY WALK IN THE GROUNDS OF THE ENGLISH ROYAL PALACE.

Note: This is a long scene, it is usually shortened considerably in productions.

PRINCE MALCOLM
Let us find a secluded spot and weep away our sorrows, Lord Macduff.

MACDUFF
I would rather take up the mighty sword, your highness, and like true men retake our fallen kingdom. Every new day, so many new widows wail, new orphans cry, and new sorrows strike at the face of heaven, that it cries out in pity for Scotland's suffering.

MALCOLM
Let us seek out some desolate shade and there
Weep our sad bosoms empty.

MACDUFF
Let us rather
Hold fast the mortal sword, and like good men
Bestride our downfall'n birthdom. Each new morn
New widows howl, new orphans cry, new sorrows
Strike heaven on the face, that it resounds
As if it felt with Scotland and yell'd out
Like syllable of dolor.

Note: Bestride – stand astride protectively over the fallen country.

PRINCE MALCOLM
(*suspicious of Macduff*) I'll mourn what I believe, and believe only what I know. That which I can put right I will, when the time is right. What you have said may well be true. This tyrant – the utterance of whose name blisters our tongues - was once thought to be honest. You yourself once thought highly of him. I see he has not harmed you yet. I am young, but have experience enough to know something of his nature, and I understand the benefit of offering up a poor, weak innocent lamb to appease an angry God.

MALCOLM
What I believe, I'll wail;
What know, believe; and what I can redress,
As I shall find the time to friend, I will.
What you have spoke, it may be so perchance.
This tyrant, whose sole name blisters our tongues,
Was once thought honest. You have loved him well;
He hath not touch'd you yet. I am young, but something
You may deserve of him through me, and wisdom
To offer up a weak, poor, innocent lamb
To appease an angry god.

MACDUFF
I am not treacherous.

MACDUFF
I am not treacherous.

Act IV Scene III. English King's Palace.

143

PRINCE MALCOLM	MALCOLM
But Macbeth is. And even a good and virtuous person may yield to the pressure of a royal command. But forgive me, my concerns cannot change who you are – angels still shine in the sky, even though the brightest has fallen. While evil wears the pretence of innocence, real innocence will look no different.	But Macbeth is. A good and virtuous nature may recoil In an imperial charge. But I shall crave your pardon; That which you are, my thoughts cannot transpose. Angels are bright still, though the brightest fell. Though all things foul would wear the brows of grace, Yet grace must still look so.

Note: Malcolm is suspicious. Macbeth has yet to harm Macduff. Malcolm is a threat to Macbeth while he lives. Macduff could win favour with Macbeth by betraying Malcolm. It would be a smart move for Macduff to offer up Malcolm like a sacrificial lamb to satisfy an angry god like Macbeth.

MACDUFF	MACDUFF
Then I have lost everything in coming here.	I have lost my hopes.

PRINCE MALCOLM	MALCOLM
Perhaps that is why I have my suspicions. Why did you leave your wife and children so vulnerable? Your most precious possessions? Abandoning such strong bonds of love? I hope you understand, my suspicions are for my own safety rather than to discredit you. You may be truly honourable, whatever I may think.	Perchance even there where I did find my doubts. Why in that rawness left you wife and child, Those precious motives, those strong knots of love, Without leave-taking? I pray you, Let not my jealousies be your dishonors, But mine own safeties. You may be rightly just, Whatever I shall think.

Note: Malcolm says it all here. What if Macduff came to England and Prince Malcolm didn't give him aid? If Macduff is genuine he could not return to Scotland or Macbeth would kill him. Why would Macduff risk everything coming to England when he wasn't sure he'd get support? Leaving his family behind suggests he planned on being able to go back again.

MACDUFF

(*in despair*) Then let our poor country bleed! Its foundations laid in evil tyranny, where all that is good dare not stand in its way.

(*about Macbeth*) Flaunt what you stole, tyrant, your title is assured!

(*to Malcolm*) Farewell, my lord, I would not be the villain you fear I am for all the land now in that tyrant's grasp, nor for all the riches in the East either.

PRINCE MALCOLM

Don't be offended. I do not completely distrust you. Our country sinks under the weight of oppression. It weeps, it bleeds, and with each new day a fresh gaping wound is added to its pains. That said, I think many hands would rise up to fight my cause – already from the gracious English king I have the offer of a good few thousand men. But all for what? When I have stamped on the evil tyrant's head, or have it upon the end of my sword, my poor country will have more lawlessness, suffering and vice than ever before under its new ruler.

MACDUFF

Who would that be?

PRINCE MALCOLM

I am referring to myself. Should all the vices lying within me be given free reign they would make the dark evil of Macbeth seem as pure as the driven snow. The poor country will think him a lamb compared to the bottomless depths of my depravity.

MACDUFF

Not even the confines of despicable hell could produce a demon more damned with evil than Macbeth.

MACDUFF

Bleed, bleed, poor country!
Great tyranny, lay thou thy basis sure,
For goodness dare not check thee. Wear thou thy wrongs;
The title is affeer'd. Fare thee well, lord.
I would not be the villain that thou think'st
For the whole space that's in the tyrant's grasp
And the rich East to boot.

MALCOLM

Be not offended;
I speak not as in absolute fear of you.
I think our country sinks beneath the yoke;
It weeps, it bleeds, and each new day a gash
Is added to her wounds. I think withal
There would be hands uplifted in my right;
And here from gracious England have I offer
Of goodly thousands. But for all this,
When I shall tread upon the tyrant's head,
Or wear it on my sword, yet my poor country
Shall have more vices than it had before,
More suffer and more sundry ways than ever,
By him that shall succeed.

MACDUFF

What should he be?

MALCOLM

It is myself I mean, in whom I know
All the particulars of vice so grafted
That, when they shall be open'd, black Macbeth
Will seem as pure as snow, and the poor state
Esteem him as a lamb, being compared
With my confineless harms.

MACDUFF

Not in the legions
Of horrid hell can come a devil more damn'd
In evils to top Macbeth.

PRINCE MALCOLM

I grant you he is a bloody, depraved, greedy, dishonest, deceitful, violent, malicious – I could include every sin under the sun – but there is no limit, none at all, to my debauchery. Your wives, your daughters, your mistresses and your innocent young maidens would not be enough to fill the foul depths of my lust. Desires so strong, they would crush all that oppose me. Better to have Macbeth reign than one such as I.

MACDUFF

Unbridled lust can consume a person. It has caused many a king's downfall and the untimely emptying of thrones. But do not fear taking upon yourself what is rightfully yours. You could discretely practice your pleasures in quiet abundance, yet still seem outwardly decent. It would be easy for you to cover up and we have plenty enough willing young ladies. The vulture in even you cannot be so great as to devour every woman willing to give themselves to the greatest catch of all.

PRINCE MALCOLM

But within my evil nature there also grows such an unquenchable greed, that, if I were king, I would execute the nobles for their lands, seize one man's jewels, another man's house, and the more I consumed, the greater my hunger would grow, even to the extent where I would invent disputes with the good and the loyal so I could destroy them solely for their wealth.

MALCOLM

I grant him bloody,
Luxurious, avaricious, false, deceitful,
Sudden, malicious, smacking of every sin
That has a name. But there's no bottom, none,
In my voluptuousness. Your wives, your
  daughters,
Your matrons, and your maids could not fill up
The cistern of my lust, and my desire
All continent impediments would o'erbear
That did oppose my will. Better Macbeth
Than such an one to reign.

MACDUFF

Boundless intemperance
In nature is a tyranny; it hath been
The untimely emptying of the happy throne,
And fall of many kings. But fear not yet
To take upon you what is yours. You may
Convey your pleasures in a spacious plenty
And yet seem cold, the time you may so
  hoodwink.
We have willing dames enough; there cannot be
That vulture in you, to devour so many
As will to greatness dedicate themselves,
Finding it so inclined.

MALCOLM

With this there grows
In my most ill-composed affection such
A stanchless avarice that, were I King,
I should cut off the nobles for their lands,
Desire his jewels and this other's house,
And my more-having would be as a sauce
To make me hunger more, that I should forge
Quarrels unjust against the good and loyal,
Destroying them for wealth.

MACDUFF

This greed is a deeper-seated problem. It grows from more destructive roots than youthful lust, and has been the sword by which many kings have met their end. Still, do not fear, Scotland has rich bounty, enough to satisfy your passion within the royal estates alone. These weaknesses are bearable when weighed against your other virtues.

PRINCE MALCOLM

But I have none. Royal virtues such as justice, honesty, restraint, consistency, generosity, steadfastness, compassion, humility, piety, patience, courage, fortitude – all absent in me. But I am abundant in every area of criminal vice, in all its forms. No, if I had power, I would pour the sweet milk of accord straight into hell, smash the universal peace, and destroy all unity on earth.

MACDUFF

Oh, Scotland, Scotland!

PRINCE MALCOLM

Tell me if such a man is fit to govern. For I am as I have said.

MACDUFF

Fit to govern? No, not fit to live! Oh wretched nation, with an untitled tyrant on a stolen, bloodied throne! When will you see virtuous days again, since the rightful heir to the throne by his own admission stands condemned and an insult to his bloodline? Your royal father was a most saintly king. The queen that bore you - more often on her knees than her feet - cleansed herself everyday through prayer. I bid you farewell! The evils you bring upon yourself have banished me from Scotland. Oh my heart, all hope ends here!

MACDUFF

This avarice

Sticks deeper, grows with more pernicious root
Than summer-seeming lust, and it hath been
The sword of our slain kings. Yet do not fear;
Scotland hath foisons to fill up your will
Of your mere own. All these are portable,
With other graces weigh'd.

MALCOLM

But I have none. The king-becoming graces,
As justice, verity, temperance, stableness,
Bounty, perseverance, mercy, lowliness,
Devotion, patience, courage, fortitude,
I have no relish of them, but abound
In the division of each several crime,
Acting it many ways. Nay, had I power, I should
Pour the sweet milk of concord into hell,
Uproar the universal peace, confound
All unity on earth.

MACDUFF

O Scotland, Scotland!

MALCOLM

If such a one be fit to govern, speak.
I am as I have spoken.

MACDUFF

Fit to govern?
No, not to live. O nation miserable!
With an untitled tyrant bloody-scepter'd,
When shalt thou see thy wholesome days again,
Since that the truest issue of thy throne
By his own interdiction stands accursed,
And does blaspheme his breed? Thy royal father
Was a most sainted king: the queen that bore
  thee,
Oftener upon her knees than on her feet,
Died every day she lived. Fare thee well!
These evils thou repeat'st upon thyself
Have banish'd me from Scotland. O my breast,
Thy hope ends here!

PRINCE MALCOLM

Macduff, this noble passion bears out your integrity, it has wiped the darkest doubts from my mind and satisfied me that your honour is good and true. The devilish Macbeth, by false pretence and deception, seeks to suppress me, so common sense restrains me from any rash decisions. But let God be our judge, for now I place myself under your direction and retract my previous statements. I hereby renounce the corruption and disgraces I laid upon myself. They are foreign to my nature. In fact, I have still as yet to lay with a woman. I have always been true to my word, rarely desiring that which was already mine, and at no time have I broken my Christian faith. I would not betray even the devil to his friend, and I have as much respect for truth as I do for life itself. This was my first untruth and it was about myself. What I truly am is yours and my poor country's servant. Before your arrival, Old Siward, with ten thousand warriors armed to the teeth, was preparing for war. Now we'll go together, our chances of success being equal to the justice of our cause! – Why the silence?

MACDUFF

So many welcome and unwelcome things heard at once. It's difficult to resolve.

MALCOLM

Macduff, this noble passion,
Child of integrity, hath from my soul
Wiped the black scruples, reconciled my thoughts
To thy good truth and honor. Devilish Macbeth
By many of these trains hath sought to win me
Into his power, and modest wisdom plucks me
From over-credulous haste. But God above
Deal between thee and me! For even now
I put myself to thy direction and
Unspeak mine own detraction; here abjure
The taints and blames I laid upon myself,
For strangers to my nature. I am yet
Unknown to woman, never was forsworn,
Scarcely have coveted what was mine own,
At no time broke my faith, would not betray
The devil to his fellow, and delight
No less in truth than life. My first false speaking
Was this upon myself. What I am truly,
Is thine and my poor country's to command:
Whither indeed, before thy here-approach,
Old Siward, with ten thousand warlike men,
Already at a point, was setting forth.
Now we'll together, and the chance of goodness
Be like our warranted quarrel! Why are you silent?

MACDUFF

Such welcome and unwelcome things at once
'Tis hard to reconcile.

A DOCTOR ARRIVES.

Note: This encounter with the doctor is often skipped in productions, but does show how the real King of England was revered and how he and the people believed him truly above mortals and chosen by God, which shows just how much more of a terrible thing in those days Macbeth's killing of the king seemed. It was also included for King James' benefit, who would be in the audience, along with the King of Denmark, which is why Shakespeare made the Vikings Norwegians instead of Danes.

Act IV Scene III. English King's Palace.

PRINCE MALCOLM
Well, more of that later.
- You, Doctor, is the King coming this way?

MALCOLM
Well, more anon. Comes the King forth, I pray you?

DOCTOR
Yes, sir. There's a crowd of wretched souls seeking his cure. Though their sickness defeats the greatest efforts of medical science, with one touch from him they are instantly cured by the power that heaven has given his hand.

DOCTOR
Ay, sir, there are a crew of wretched souls
That stay his cure. Their malady convinces
The great assay of art, but at his touch,
Such sanctity hath heaven given his hand,
They presently amend.

PRINCE MALCOLM
I thank you, Doctor.

MALCOLM
I thank you, Doctor.

THE DOCTOR LEAVES.

MACDUFF
What sickness does he mean?

MACDUFF
What's the disease he means?

PRINCE MALCOLM
The sickness known as the *King's Evil*. This good King has a most miraculous gift, I've seen him use it often since I came to England. How he invokes heaven, only he knows, but he cures people with the strangest of ailments, all swollen and ulcerous and pitiful to look at, completely beyond the help of surgery. He hangs a gold coin around their neck and blesses them with holy prayers. It's said his healing power will be handed down to succeeding monarchs, and along with this rare gift he also has of the divine gift of prophecy. Heaven has truly blessed him with the grace of God.

MALCOLM
'Tis call'd the evil:
A most miraculous work in this good King,
Which often, since my here-remain in England,
I have seen him do. How he solicits heaven,
Himself best knows; but strangely-visited people,
All swol'n and ulcerous, pitiful to the eye,
The mere despair of surgery, he cures,
Hanging a golden stamp about their necks,
Put on with holy prayers: and 'tis spoken,
To the succeeding royalty he leaves
The healing benediction. With this strange virtue
He hath a heavenly gift of prophecy,
And sundry blessings hang about his throne
That speak him full of grace.

Note: The King and the people of the day truly believed the King had the power granted by God to cure diseases with just the touch of his hand. The skin disease Scrofula was known as the 'King's Evil', as the King was thought to be the only cure from it. Even touching the image of the King's head on a gold coin was thought to help right up until the 18th Century.

ENTER LORD ROSS.

MACDUFF
Look who has arrived.

MACDUFF
See, who comes here?

PRINCE MALCOLM
A fellow countryman by his dress, but I don't recognise him.

MACDUFF
My good cousin, Ross. Welcome. Join us.

PRINCE MALCOLM
Yes, I recognize him now. May the good Lord speedily repair that which makes us strangers!

LORD ROSS
Sir, amen to that.

MACDUFF
Is Scotland still as it was?

LORD ROSS
Alas, poor country, almost unrecognisable now! It's not the land of our birth anymore, but the land of our death. A place where only ignorant fools are seen to smile, where the sighs and groans and shrieks that fill the air go unheeded. Where violence and sorrow are so commonplace people no longer ask for whom the funeral bell tolls, and where good men's lives expire before the flowers in their caps, sickness and old age no longer claiming them.

MACDUFF
Oh, cousin, too sad, and sadly all too true.

PRINCE MALCOLM
What is the latest grief?

LORD ROSS
News an hour old is already old news. Every minute brings fresh new grief.

MACDUFF
How is my wife?

LORD ROSS
She's well.

MACDUFF
And my children?

LORD ROSS
Well too.

MALCOLM
My countryman: but yet I know him not.

MACDUFF
My ever gentle cousin, welcome hither.

MALCOLM
I know him now. Good God, betimes remove
The means that makes us strangers!

ROSS
Sir, amen.

MACDUFF
Stands Scotland where it did?

ROSS
Alas, poor country,
Almost afraid to know itself! It cannot
Be call'd our mother, but our grave. Where nothing,
But who knows nothing, is once seen to smile;
Where sighs and groans and shrieks that rend the air,
Are made, not mark'd; where violent sorrow seems
A modern ecstasy. The dead man's knell
Is there scarce ask'd for who, and good men's lives
Expire before the flowers in their caps,
Dying or ere they sicken.

MACDUFF
O, relation
Too nice, and yet too true!

MALCOLM
What's the newest grief?

ROSS
That of an hour's age doth hiss the speaker;
Each minute teems a new one.

MACDUFF
How does my wife?

ROSS
Why, well.

MACDUFF
And all my children?

ROSS
Well too.

MACDUFF

That tyrant has not disturbed their peace?

LORD ROSS

No, they were at peace when I left them.

MACDUFF

Don't hold back with your words. How are they really?

LORD ROSS

As I came here to deliver the news which I have borne with heavy heart, there were rumours of many capable men taking up arms, which I can believe as I witnessed for myself the tyrant's army on the move. Now more than ever, we need aid.

(*turning to Malcolm*) Prince Malcolm, your presence in Scotland would persuade men to take up arms. Even the women would join the fight to throw off their desperate suffering.

PRINCE MALCOLM

They may take comfort, we are on our way. The gracious English king has lent us the honourable Siward, Earl of Northumberland, with ten thousand men under his command. There is no soldier more experienced or wiser in the whole of Christendom.

LORD ROSS

If only I could return this comforting news with some of my own. But I have news fit only to be howled into the desert air, where no living soul could hear it.

MACDUFF

(*concerned*) Concerning what? News in general or bad news carried for one person in particular?

MACDUFF

The tyrant has not batter'd at their peace?

ROSS

No; they were well at peace when I did leave 'em.

MACDUFF

Be not a niggard of your speech. How goes't?

ROSS

When I came hither to transport the tidings,
Which I have heavily borne, there ran a rumor
Of many worthy fellows that were out,
Which was to my belief witness'd the rather,
For that I saw the tyrant's power a-foot:
Now is the time of help; your eye in Scotland
Would create soldiers, make our women fight,
To doff their dire distresses.

MALCOLM

Be't their comfort
We are coming thither. Gracious England hath
Lent us good Siward and ten thousand men;
An older and a better soldier none
That Christendom gives out.

ROSS:

Would I could answer
This comfort with the like! But I have words
That would be howl'd out in the desert air,
Where hearing should not latch them.

MACDUFF

What concern they?
The general cause? Or is it a fee-grief
Due to some single breast?

Note: Macduff knows what news is likely. He is dreading hearing it.

LORD ROSS Any decent man would grieve at such news, however the main part relates to you alone.	ROSS No mind that's honest But in it shares some woe, though the main part Pertains to you alone.
MACDUFF If it is my news, don't keep it from me, tell me at once.	MACDUFF If it be mine, Keep it not from me, quickly let me have it.
LORD ROSS Let your ears not forever despise my tongue when it delivers to them the gravest sound they ever heard.	ROSS Let not your ears despise my tongue for ever, Which shall possess them with the heaviest sound That ever yet they heard.
MACDUFF Hmm! I can guess what it is.	MACDUFF Humh! I guess at it.
LORD ROSS Your castle was attacked...	ROSS Your castle is surprised;

MACDUFF FREEZES, FEARING WHAT HE KNOWS IS COMING.

LORD ROSS (CONT'D) ...Your wife and children, savagely slaughtered... To relate the details of your loved ones' brutal deaths would only serve to add your body to the count.	ROSS Your castle is surprised; your wife and babes Savagely slaughter'd. To relate the manner Were, on the quarry of these murder'd deer, To add the death of you.

MACDUFF COVERS HIS FACE WITH HIS HANDS, STRICKEN WITH GRIEF.

PRINCE MALCOLM Heaven have mercy! (*to Macduff*) What, man! Don't cover your eyes; voice your sorrow. Silent grief whispers inwardly to the already overburdened heart, stretching it to breaking point.	MALCOLM Merciful heaven! What, man! Ne'er pull your hat upon your brows; Give sorrow words. The grief that does not speak Whispers the o'er fraught heart, and bids it break.
MACDUFF My children too?	MACDUFF My children too?
LORD ROSS Wife, children, servants, anyone they could find.	ROSS Wife, children, servants, all That could be found.
MACDUFF And I had to be away at the time! My wife killed too?	MACDUFF And I must be from thence! My wife kill'd too?
LORD ROSS As I have said.	ROSS I have said.

PRINCE MALCOLM

Be assured, our great revenge shall be the medicine to take comfort in and cure this deadly grief.

MALCOLM

Be comforted.
Let's make us medicines of our great revenge,
To cure this deadly grief.

MACDUFF

(*distraught*) He has no children! All my pretty young ones? Did you say all? Sadistic beast! All? All my pretty chicks and their mother in one fell swoop?

MACDUFF

He has no children. All my pretty ones?
Did you say all? O hell-kite! All?
What, all my pretty chickens and their dam
At one fell swoop?

> Note: 'Fell swoop' signifies a bird of prey swooping (diving) down to catch its prey. The word 'fell' used to mean evil, ruthless and destructive, from which we get the word 'felon'. Today the expression has mellowed to mean 'all at once'.

PRINCE MALCOLM

Face it like a man, Macduff.

MALCOLM

Dispute it like a man.

MACDUFF

I shall do. But a man has feelings. I can't just forget things that were so precious to me. Did heaven look down upon this and not help them?
(*to self*) Sinful Macduff! They were killed because of you – worthless as I am - not for their sins were they slaughtered, but for mine. God rest their souls in peace!

MACDUFF:

I shall do so;
But I must also feel it as a man.
I cannot but remember such things were,
That were most precious to me. Did heaven look
   on,
And would not take their part? Sinful Macduff,
They were all struck for thee! Naught that I am,
Not for their own demerits, but for mine,
Fell slaughter on their souls. Heaven rest them
   now!

PRINCE MALCOLM

Let this hone your sword. Turn your grief to anger; be not dull of heart, enrage it!

MALCOLM

Be this the whetstone of your sword. Let grief
Convert to anger; blunt not the heart, enrage it.

MACDUFF

Oh, I could cry womanly tears with my eyes, and rant with my tongue, but, by heavens, there's no time for that!

MACDUFF

O, I could play the woman with mine eyes,
And braggart with my tongue! But, gentle heavens,
Cut short all intermission;

MACDUFF STARTS PULLING HIMSELF TOGETHER,
HIS GRIEF TURNING INTO A DESIRE FOR REVENGE.

MACDUFF (CONT'D)

(*defiant*) Bring this fiend of Scotland face to face with me within my sword's reach. If he escapes, may heaven forgive us both!

MACDUFF

front to front
Bring thou this fiend of Scotland and myself;
Within my sword's length set him; if he 'scape,
Heaven forgive him too!

PRINCE MALCOLM

Spoken like a man. Come, we'll go to the King. Our army is ready, all we need do is leave. Macbeth is ripe for the taking and the powers above will guide us in our quest.

Take heart, and receive what comfort you may,

Even the longest night finds the new day.

MALCOLM

This tune goes manly.

Come, go we to the King; our power is ready;

Our lack is nothing but our leave. Macbeth

Is ripe for shaking, and the powers above

Put on their instruments. Receive what cheer you may;

The night is long that never finds the day.

Historical Note:

James VI of Scotland (who was confusingly also James I of England) married princess Anne of Denmark (though James didn't attend the ceremony). She sailed for Scotland to be with her new husband, but was driven back by storms which were blamed on scheming witches. Not to be beaten, King James set sail to Denmark to meet his new bride. Returning to Scotland King James was battered by storms at sea. This he blamed on a group of Scottish witches. James himself oversaw the interrogation of these so called witches and became convinced that they had tried to kill him by raising storms, moulding wax images of him, and by making poison to use against him.

King James wrote a paper called 'Daemonologie' based on what he had learnt from the trials about witchcraft. He wanted to show he was a leading expert in the field and to convert non believers to his beliefs.

It is believed James VI and his father-in-law, the King of Denmark, attended a special performance of Macbeth together. Hence Shakespeare weaving so many topical events into a story which was based on historical events almost 500 years before the play was written.

End of Act IV

ACT V

THE BEGINNING OF THE END

I'LL NOT BE AFRAID OF DEATH AND PAIN,
TILL BIRNAM WOOD COMES TO DUNSINANE

ACT V

ACT V SCENE I

A BEDCHAMBER IN CASTLE DUNSINANE.

A LADY-IN-WAITING SITS IN LADY MACBETH'S LARGE BEDCHAMBER. SHE
HAS NODDED OFF TO SLEEP. LADY MACBETH IS ASLEEP IN HER BED.

A DOCTOR ENTERS WITH TWO HOT DRINKS. THE LADY-IN-WAITING WAKES
WITH A START, PRETENDING SHE WAS NOT ASLEEP. SHE TAKES THE DRINK
OFFERED HER. IT LOOKS AS IF IT HAS BEEN A LONG WAIT.

THE DOCTOR SETTLES IN HIS CHAIR WITH HIS DRINK.

> Note: Shakespeare wrote the lines for this scene in prose, signifying Lady
> Macbeth's decline into madness.

DOCTOR
(*low voice*) For two nights I've watched with you, but still see no truth in your report. When was it you say she last walked in her sleep?

LADY-IN-WAITING
Since his Majesty went to war, I've seen her rise from her bed, throw on her nightgown, unlock her desk, take out paper, fold it, write on it, read it, then seal it and return again to bed, doctor. Yet all the while still deep in sleep.

DOCTOR
(*quietly*) If defies nature, to receive the benefit of sleep while carrying out the tasks of the waking! In this restless slumber, besides her walking and other actions, have you heard her say anything?

LADY-IN-WAITING
Only things I could not repeat, doctor.

DOCTOR
I have two nights watched with you, but can perceive no truth in your report. When was it she last walked?

GENTLEWOMAN
Since his Majesty went into the field, I have seen her rise from her bed, throw her nightgown upon her, unlock her closet, take forth paper, fold it, write upon't, read it, afterwards seal it, and again return to bed; yet all this while in a most fast sleep.

DOCTOR
A great perturbation in nature, to receive at once the benefit of sleep and do the effects of watching! In this slumbery agitation, besides her walking and other actual performances, what, at any time, have you heard her say?

GENTLEWOMAN
That, sir, which I will not report after her.

DOCTOR
You may to me, it's most important that you do.

LADY-IN-WAITING
Not to you or to anyone, without a witness to back me up.

DOCTOR
You may to me, and 'tis most meet you should.

GENTLEWOMAN
Neither to you nor any one, having no witness to confirm my speech.

> *Note: She has heard Lady Macbeth talking of her part in the killing of King Duncan. She daren't retell it without someone to confirm her words, or she would be in danger of the accusation of spreading malicious rumours about the Queen and thereby would be killed herself. As has been said earlier, these were dangerous times.*

LADY MACBETH STANDS AND HEADS TOWARDS A DRESSING TABLE. SHE CARRIES A LIGHTED CANDLE WHICH SHE PLACES ON THE TABLE.

SHE WIPES HER HANDS ON HER GOWN ANXIOUSLY.

LADY-IN-WAITING (CONT'D)
Look. Here she comes now, and upon my life, fast asleep just as I described. Watch her, but don't let her see you.

DOCTOR
Where did she get the light?

LADY-IN-WAITING
It stands bedside her bed. She has light continually, it is her order.

DOCTOR
Do you see? Her eyes are open.

LADY-IN-WAITING
Aye, but to sight they are shut.

GENTLEWOMAN
Lo you, here she comes! This is her very guise, and, upon my life, fast asleep. Observe her; stand close.

DOCTOR
How came she by that light?

GENTLEWOMAN
Why, it stood by her. She has light by her continually; 'tis her command.

DOCTOR
You see, her eyes are open.

GENTLEWOMAN
Ay, but their sense is shut.

LADY MACBETH CONTINUALLY GOES THROUGH THE ACTION OF WASHING HER HANDS, BUT CANNOT GET RID OF THE IMAGINARY STAINS, NOR THE SMELL OF THE BLOOD FROM WHEN SHE RETURNED THE DAGGERS AFTER THE MURDER OF KING DUNCAN.

DOCTOR
What is she doing now? See, she is rubbing her hands.

LADY-IN-WAITING
It's something she does often, as if she is washing her hands. I have known her do this for a full quarter of an hour.

LADY MACBETH
(*at her hands*) Still there's a spot!

DOCTOR
What is it she does now? Look how she rubs her hands.

GENTLEWOMAN
It is an accustomed action with her, to seem thus washing her hands. I have known her continue in this a quarter of an hour.

LADY MACBETH
Yet here's a spot.

DOCTOR

Listen! She speaks. I'll make a note of what she says to ensure I remember it correctly.

DOCTOR

Hark, she speaks! I will set down what comes from her, to satisfy my remembrance the more strongly.

THE DOCTOR TAKES A QUILL FROM THE DESK BESIDE HIM.
HE STARTS WRITING.

LADY MACBETH

Out, damned spot! Out, I say! -

LADY MACBETH

Out, damned spot! Out, I say!

LADY MACBETH STOPS AND LISTENS AND COUNTS AN IMAGINARY BELL.

LADY MACBETH (CONT'D)

One... Two... It's time to do it.
(*she shivers*) Hell is dark and dismal!
(*strong again*) Pah, my lord, pah! A soldier afraid? Why fear who knows? Our power is now so great no one can question our actions.
(*weaker*) Yet who'd have thought the old man had so much blood in him?

LADY MACBETH

One–two— why then 'tis time to do't.
Hell is murky.
Fie, my lord, fie! A soldier, and afeard? What need we fear who knows it, when none can call our power to account? Yet who would have thought the old man to have had so much blood in him?

DOCTOR

Did you hear that?

DOCTOR

Do you mark that?

HE SCRIBBLES AWAY FRANTICALLY TRYING TO KEEP UP.

LADY MACBETH

(*like a nursery rhyme*) The Lord of Fife he had a wife...
(*ominous*) Where is she now? –

LADY MACBETH

The Thane of Fife had a wife; where is she now?

SHE LAUGHS AN EVIL LAUGH, THEN STOPS, STARING AT HER HANDS.

LADY MACBETH (CONT'D)

What? Will these hands never be clean?

LADY MACBETH

What, will these hands ne'er be clean?

SHE RECALLS THE BANQUET WITH THE GHOST OF BANQUO.

LADY MACBETH (CONT'D)

No more of this madness, my lord, no more. You'll ruin everything with your fearful fits.

LADY MACBETH

No more o' that, my lord, no more o' that. You mar all with this starting.

DOCTOR

(*to Lady-in-Waiting, looking up from his writing*) My, my, you have heard things you shouldn't have.

DOCTOR

Go to, go to; you have known what you should not.

LADY-IN-WAITING
She's said things she shouldn't have, I'm sure of that. Heaven knows what else she knows.

GENTLEWOMAN
She has spoke what she should not, I am sure of that. Heaven knows what she has known.

LADY MACBETH STOPS WASHING HER HANDS AND HOLDS ONE UP TO HER FACE, SNIFFING IT.

LADY MACBETH
Still the smell of blood. All the perfumes in Arabia could not sweeten this one little hand.

LADY MACBETH
Here's the smell of the blood still. All the perfumes of Arabia will not sweeten this little hand.

SHE SIGHS DEEPLY.

LADY MACBETH (CONT'D)
(*forlornly*) Oh! Oh! Oh!

LADY MACBETH
Oh, oh, oh!

DOCTOR
What a sigh! Her heart is sorely burdened.

DOCTOR
What a sigh is there! The heart is sorely charged.

LADY-IN-WAITING
I would not wish for such a heart in my bosom, queen or no queen.

GENTLEWOMAN
I would not have such a heart in my bosom for the dignity of the whole body.

DOCTOR
(*finishing writing*) Well, well, well...

DOCTOR
Well, well, well—

LADY-IN-WAITING
Pray God it will be 'well', doctor.

GENTLEWOMAN
Pray God it be, sir.

THE DOCTOR CHECKS BACK THROUGH HIS WRITING.

DOCTOR
This disease is beyond my experience. I have known sleep-walkers, but they all died in their beds with a clear conscience.

DOCTOR
This disease is beyond my practice. Yet I have known those which have walked in their sleep who have died holily in their beds.

LADY MACBETH LOOKS OVER AT THE DOCTOR AS IF HEARING HIM. SHE SPEAKS TO THE DOCTOR AS IF HE IS MACBETH.

LADY MACBETH
(*to an imaginary Macbeth*) Wash your hands, put on your night gown, don't look so afraid. I've told you before – Banquo's buried, he cannot rise from his grave.

LADY MACBETH
Wash your hands, put on your nightgown; look not so pale. I tell you yet again, Banquo's buried; he cannot come out on's grave.

DOCTOR
(*the truth dawning on him*) Is that so?

DOCTOR
Even so?

THE DOCTOR'S VOICE FREEZES LADY MACBETH.

REACTING TO THE NOISE, SHAKING AND FRIGHTENED, SHE TAKES THE
DOCTOR'S HAND AND LEADS HIM TO HER BED.

LADY MACBETH
To bed, to bed...
(*pausing*) There's knocking at the gate!
Come, come, come... Come, give me your
hand. What's done cannot be undone. To
bed, to bed, to bed...

LADY MACBETH
To bed, to bed; there's knocking at the gate.
Come, come, come, come, give me your hand.
What's done cannot be undone. To bed, to
bed, to bed.

DOCTOR
(*hushed, to Lady-in-Waiting*) Will she go
back to bed now?

DOCTOR
Will she go now to bed?

LADY-IN-WAITING
Yes, right away.

GENTLEWOMAN
Directly.

LADY MACBETH LEADS THE DOCTOR BACK TO HER BED,
WHICH SHE CLIMBS INTO.

SOMEWHAT SHAKEN BY THE EXPERIENCE, THE DOCTOR
THEN HEADS BACK TO THE LADY-IN-WAITING.

DOCTOR
There are whispers on the street of foul
goings-on. And unnatural deeds bring
about unnatural troubles – like infected
minds whispering their secrets to deaf
pillows. She's more in need of a priest
than a physician. God, help us all! Look
after her, remove anything she could use
to harm herself...

DOCTOR
Foul whisperings are abroad. Unnatural deeds
Do breed unnatural troubles: infected minds
To their deaf pillows will discharge their secrets:
More needs she the divine than the physician.
God, God, forgive us all! Look after her;
Remove from her the means of all annoyance,

HE TURNS TO LEAVE.

DOCTOR (CONT'D)
...and keep a close watch on her.
And so goodnight, I'll say my goodbyes
She's baffled my brain and amazed my eyes.
I daren't say what I think of it all.

DOCTOR
And still keep eyes upon her. So good night:
My mind she has mated, and amazed my sight:
I think, but dare not speak.

HE HEADS HURRIEDLY FOR THE DOOR.

LADY-IN-WAITING
Good night, good doctor.

GENTLEWOMAN
Good night, good doctor.

Act V Scene I. Bedchamber In Castle Dunsinane.

ELSEWHERE IN THE CASTLE, LORDS AND FOLLOWERS OF MACBETH ARE
FLEEING FROM DUNSINANE CASTLE. ALL ABANDONING THE EVER
MADDENING MACBETH.

Note: The is the last appearance of Lady Macbeth. She speaks this scene in prose, unusual for a scene of tragedy and even more unusually, the only of Shakespeare's great tragic characters not given the dignity of exiting in verse.

Switching to prose from verse was a trick used by Shakespeare for madness. Hamlet, when feigning madness, spoke in prose, other times in verse, Ophelia in her madness sang or spoke in prose and King Lear spoke in prose when mad, then back to verse when he recovered.

ACT V SCENE II

A Secret Place Near Dunsinane.

A secret meeting of the Scottish Lords is taking place at the edge of a wood between Menteith, Angus, Lennox and Caithness.

MENTEITH
The English forces are near, led by Malcolm, with his uncle Siward and the honourable Macduff in support. Revenge burns in them so passionately even the dead would rise up in support.

MENTEITH
The English power is near, led on by Malcolm,
His uncle Siward, and the good Macduff.
Revenges burn in them, for their dear causes
Would to the bleeding and the grim alarm
Excite the mortified man.

Note: In Holinshed's inaccurate history (Shakespeare's historical source) Siward is the father-in-law of King Duncan and therefore the grandfather of Malcolm.

ANGUS
They're coming via Birnam Wood. We can meet them there.

ANGUS
Near Birnam Wood Shall we well meet them; that way are they coming.

CAITHNESS
Has anyone heard if Donalbain is with his brother?

CAITHNESS
Who knows if Donalbain be with his brother?

LORD LENNOX
I know for certain he is not. I have a list of the gentry supporting the uprising. Siward's son is there with many whisker-less youths fighting for their first time.

LENNOX
For certain, sir, he is not; I have a file
Of all the gentry. There is Siward's son
And many unrough youths, that even now
Protest their first of manhood.

MENTEITH
What is the tyrant doing?

MENTEITH
What does the tyrant?

CAITHNESS
He has strongly fortified Great Dunsinane Castle. Some say he's mad, others who despise him less call it valiant fury. But one thing is certain, he has lost all control.

CAITHNESS
Great Dunsinane he strongly fortifies.
Some say he's mad; others, that lesser hate him,
Do call it valiant fury: but, for certain,
He cannot buckle his distemper'd cause
Within the belt of rule.

Note: 'Buckle his distempered cause' - cannot control himself or his people. Imagine a man with a large belly vainly trying to do up his belt.

Act V Scene II. A Secret Meeting Place.

ANGUS

Now he feels the blood of the murders he's concealed sticking to his hands. Every minute new uprisings rebel against his abuse of power. Those he commands obey only from duty, not from respect. Now he feels his title hanging loosely about him, like a giant's robe on a dwarven thief.

MENTEITH

Who can blame his afflicted mind for rebelling against him, when his soul itself is ashamed to be a part of him?

CAITHNESS

Well, let us march onwards to give allegiance where it is truly owed. We'll meet Malcolm, the cure to this sickening disease, and with him shed every last drop of our blood to purge this country of its ills.

LORD LENNOX

With ev'ry drop, or as much blood as it
  needs,
To wet the sovereign flower and drown the
  weeds.
We march to Birnam!

ANGUS

Now does he feel
His secret murders sticking on his hands,
Now minutely revolts upbraid his faith-breach;
Those he commands move only in command,
Nothing in love. Now does he feel his title
Hang loose about him, like a giant's robe
Upon a dwarfish thief.

MENTEITH

Who then shall blame
His pester'd senses to recoil and start,
When all that is within him does condemn
Itself for being there?

CAITHNESS

Well, march we on,
To give obedience where 'tis truly owed.
Meet we the medicine of the sickly weal,
And with him pour we, in our country's purge,
Each drop of us.

LENNOX

Or so much as it needs
To dew the sovereign flower and drown the weeds.
Make we our march towards Birnam.

THEY MARCH OFF.

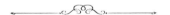

ACT V SCENE III

THE COURT OF CASTLE DUNSINANE.

MACBETH STANDS AT THE WINDOW SEEING THE PEOPLE FLEEING THE CASTLE. HE TURNS TO THE ROOM. A NUMBER OF REMAINING LORDS AND OTHER STAFF ARE PRESENT.

A MESSENGER RUSHES IN AND PASSES MACBETH A MESSAGE. MACBETH READS IT, THEN SCRUNCHES IT UP.

MACBETH
Bring me no more reports!

MACBETH
Bring me no more reports;

MACBETH FORCES THE MESSAGE INTO THE MOUTH OF THE MESSENGER WHO TURNS AND FLEES.

MACBETH (CONT'D)
Let them all flee!

MACBETH
let them fly all!

MACBETH LOOKS AT THE LORDS STILL PRESENT AS ONE BY ONE THEY TURN AND LEAVE, LOOKING AT HIM AS IF SHUNNING A MAD MAN.

MACBETH SHOUTS AFTER THEM DEFIANTLY.

MACBETH (CONT'D)
Until Birnam Wood uproots to Dunsinane I've nothing to fear! Who is this boy, Malcolm? Is he not born of woman? The spirits who know our fate have told me;
"Fear not, Macbeth; no man born of woman shall ever have power over you."

MACBETH
Till Birnam Wood remove to Dunsinane I cannot taint with fear. What's the boy Malcolm? Was he not born of woman? The spirits that know All mortal consequences have pronounced me
thus:
"Fear not, Macbeth; no man that's born of woman Shall e'er have power upon thee."

Note: Macbeth refers to Malcolm as 'the boy'. This is either as an insult, or because in Holinshed's history it refers to Malcolm as not being of an age to inherit the crown at the time Duncan was killed.

HE PACES THE ROOM THEN CROSSES TO THE WINDOW, WHERE HE CAN SEE THE LORDS MAKING PREPARATIONS TO LEAVE.

MACBETH (CONT'D)

So flee, traitors, and mingle with the English *bon vivants*! The heart and mind *I'm* ruled by shall never crumble with doubt or tremble in fear.

MACBETH

Then fly, false thanes,
And mingle with the English epicures!
The mind I sway by and the heart I bear
Shall never sag with doubt nor shake with fear.

> Note: 'Epicure' – one who liked to live and dine extravagantly. It was believed the Scots lived a more simple life and despised the perceived opulent English.

A SERVANT ENTERS LOOKING NERVOUS.
MACBETH STORMS TOWARDS HIM.

MACBETH (CONT'D)

The devil damn you, you pale faced moron!

MACBETH

The devil damn thee black, thou cream-faced loon!

MACBETH STRIKES HIM ABOUT THE FACE WITH THE BACK OF HIS HAND. HE FALLS DOWN. AS HE STANDS AGAIN MACBETH CARRIES ON HIS RANT.

MACBETH (CONT'D)

Well? Why the fearful goose face?

MACBETH

Where got'st thou that goose look?

SERVANT

(*terrified, stammering*) Th-there's ten th-th-thousand...

SERVANT

There is ten thousand—

MACBETH

(*interrupting*) What? Geese, imbecile?

MACBETH

Geese, villain?

MACBETH STRIKES HIM AGAIN.

SERVANT

S-soldiers, sir.

SERVANT

Soldiers, sir.

MACBETH

Go stab your face to colour your fear you lily livered whelp. What soldiers, fool?

MACBETH

Go prick thy face and over-red thy fear,
Thou lily-liver'd boy. What soldiers, patch?

THE SERVANT IS SO TERRIFIED HE CANNOT SPEAK. MACBETH GRABS THE SERVANT'S EAR AND PULLS HIS HEAD BACK VIOLENTLY.

MACBETH (CONT'D)

Damn your soul! Those ashen cheeks of yours will spread fear among the others. What soldiers, sallow face?

MACBETH

Death of thy soul! Those linen cheeks of thine
Are counselors to fear.
What soldiers, whey-face?

SERVANT

Th-the E-English army, if you please, sir.

SERVANT

The English force, so please you.

MACBETH PUSHES THE SERVANT TO THE FLOOR.

MACBETH	MACBETH
Remove your face from my presence.	Take thy face hence.

THE SERVANT GETS UP AND RUNS FOR HIS LIFE. THE OTHER ATTENDANTS
FOLLOW HIM OUT. MACBETH IS NOW ALONE IN THE ROOM.

MACBETH (CONT'D)	MACBETH
(*calling*) Seton!	Seyton

MACBETH CROSSES TO THE WINDOW AGAIN.
HE SEES MORE PEOPLE FLEEING.

Note: Macbeth now speaks his sixth soliloquy.

MACBETH (CONT'D)	MACBETH
(*aside*) It sickens my heart to see...	- I am sick at heart,
(*calling*) Seton, where are you!	When I behold - Seyton, I say!

MACBETH PONDERS HIS SITUATION REALISING IT IS HIS FINAL STAND, YET
STILL BELIEVING HE IS INVINCIBLE BECAUSE OF THE WITCHES PROPHECY.

MACBETH (CONT'D)	MACBETH
(*aside again*) The final battle to decide my fate one way or the other. I've lived long enough anyway. My life withers and falls now, like an autumn leaf. All that should accompany old age - honour, love, obedience, old friends - I cannot hope to have now. Instead, I have silent curses, not voiced, but held deep inside, and false praises, spoken from fear, not from the heart.	- This push Will chair me ever or disseat me now. I have lived long enough. My way of life Is fall'n into the sear, the yellow leaf, And that which should accompany old age, As honor, love, obedience, troops of friends, I must not look to have; but, in their stead, Curses, not loud but deep, mouth-honor, breath, Which the poor heart would fain deny and dare not.
(*calling angrily*) Seton!	- Seyton!

Note: 'Chair me ever or disseat me' – Macbeth will stay king for life or he will lose
the throne (and his life). This battle will decide his future.

SETON ENTERS. UNLIKE THE OTHERS, HE IS QUIETLY CONFIDENT AND
COMPOSED AROUND MACBETH'S MADNESS. THE SECRETS HE KNOWS
OFFERS HIM SOME PROTECTION.

SETON	SEYTON
What is your majesty's pleasure?	What's your gracious pleasure?

MACBETH	**MACBETH**
Any more news?	What news more?
SETON	**SEYTON**
Only confirmation, my lord, of that which has already been reported.	All is confirm'd, my lord, which was reported.
MACBETH	**MACBETH**
I'll fight till the flesh is hacked from my bones. Get me my armour.	I'll fight, 'til from my bones my flesh be hack'd. Give me my armour.
SETON	**SEYTON**
It's not needed yet.	'Tis not needed yet.
MACBETH	**MACBETH**
I'll put it on now. Send out more horsemen, scour the land. Hang any that talk of fear. Now get me my armour!	I'll put it on. Send out more horses, skirr the country round, Hang those that talk of fear. Give me mine armor.

THE DOCTOR ENTERS AS SETON LEAVES TO GET THE ARMOUR.

MACBETH	**MACBETH**
How is your patient, doctor?	How does your patient, doctor?
DOCTOR	**DOCTOR**
Not so much sick, my lord, as troubled by persistent hallucinations that keep her from sleeping.	Not so sick, my lord, As she is troubled with thick-coming fancies, That keep her from her rest.
MACBETH	**MACBETH**
Then cure her of them. Can you not treat a diseased mind? Pluck a deep rooted sorrow from the memory? Erase worries embedded in a troubled brain, and with some sweet, numbing sedative cleanse a bosom stuffed with the treacherous thoughts that weigh so heavily upon the heart?	Cure her of that. Canst thou not minister to a mind diseased, Pluck from the memory a rooted sorrow, Raze out the written troubles of the brain, And with some sweet oblivious antidote Cleanse the stuff'd bosom of that perilous stuff Which weighs upon the heart?
DOCTOR	**DOCTOR**
For such ailments the cure is with the patient himself.	Therein the patient Must minister to himself.

SETON AND A SERVANT RETURN CARRYING ARMOUR NOISILY.

MACBETH	MACBETH
Then throw your medicine to the dogs, it's of no use to me.	Throw physic to the dogs, I'll none of it.
(*to Servants*) Come, put my armour on, give me my sword.	Come, put mine armor on; give me my staff.
- Seton, send for the latest news.	Seyton, send out.

SETON NODS TO THE SERVANT, WHO NERVOUSLY LOOKS AROUND HOPING IT IS SOMEONE ELSE SETON MEANS. THE SERVANT RELUCTANTLY LEAVES TO GET NEWS (BRINGING MACBETH NEWS IS A PERILOUS JOB NOW).

MACBETH (CONT'D)	MACBETH
Doctor, the lords flee me.	Doctor, the thanes fly from me.
(*to Seton*) Come on, Seton, hurry up.	Come, sir, dispatch.

SETON PUTS THE ARMOUR ON MACBETH MORE ROUGHLY.

MACBETH (CONT'D)	MACBETH
Doctor, if you could diagnose my country's ills, purge the disease and nurse it back to sound and pristine health, I would applaud you and then echo my applause with even more applause.	If thou couldst, doctor, cast The water of my land, find her disease And purge it to a sound and pristine health, I would applaud thee to the very echo, That should applaud again.

Note: 'Cast the water' - patients were diagnosed by inspecting their urine.

THE DOCTOR LOOKS AT MACBETH ODDLY.

MACBETH SUDDENLY CHANGES HIS MIND AND DEMANDS SETON TAKE THE ARMOUR OFF.

MACBETH (CONT'D)	MACBETH
(*to Seton*) I've changed my mind. Take it off.	Pull't off, I say.
(*to Doctor*) Doctor, what herb or laxative drug would cleanse this country of the English? You've heard of them?	What rhubarb, senna, or what purgative drug Would scour these English hence? Hear'st thou of them?
DOCTOR	DOCTOR
Aye, my good lord. Your majesty's preparations bring them to our attention.	Ay, my good lord: your royal preparation Makes us hear something.

Note: The two previous speeches are ambiguous. Macbeth probably means 'have you heard of such a drug', but it would seem the doctor misunderstands and assumes he meant 'have you heard of the English'.

Act V Scene III. Castle Dunsinane.

MACBETH WAVES SETON AND THE ARMOUR AWAY.

MACBETH (CONT'D)	MACBETH
(*to Seton*) Seton, follow me with my armour.	Bring it after me.
I'll not be afraid of death and pain,	*I will not be afraid of death and bane*
Till Birnam Wood comes to Dunsinane.	*Till Birnam Forest come to Dunsinane.*

MACBETH STORMS OUT, LEAVING THE DOCTOR SUSPECTING BOTH MACBETH AND HIS WIFE ARE EQUALLY AFFLICTED.

DOCTOR	DOCTOR
(to self)	*Were I from Dunsinane away and clear,*
Were I far away from Dunsinane,	*Profit again should hardly draw me here.*
No gold could draw me back again.	

NOT FAR FROM THE CASTLE THE ENGLISH ARMY STOPS BEFORE A WOOD.

IN THE CASTLE COURTYARD, LENNOX AND CAITHNESS MOUNT AND RIDE OUT TOWARDS THAT SAME WOOD.

ACT V SCENE IV

THE COUNTRYSIDE NEAR BIRNAM WOOD.

LENNOX, CAITHNESS, MENTEITH, ROSS AND ANGUS MEET THE
ADVANCING ARMY OF PRINCE MALCOLM, SIWARD, MACDUFF,
SIWARD'S SON, AND FOOT SOLDIERS.

PRINCE MALCOLM
Fellow countrymen, I hope the day is near at hand that beds may once again be safe to sleep in.

MENTEITH
We are in no doubt about it.

SIWARD
What wood is this before us?

MENTEITH
Birnam Wood.

PRINCE MALCOLM
Tell every soldier to cut down a branch to carry before him. It will conceal the number of troops and ensure his observers report back in error.

SOLDIER
It shall be done.

SIWARD
(*to Malcolm*) Reports suggest the tyrant is confident he can stay put in Dunsinane Castle and endure our siege.

PRINCE MALCOLM
It's his only hope. When there is opportunity, his officers and men desert him. Now only lowly conscripts serve him, and their hearts aren't in it.

MACDUFF
Let's not pass judgement before the event, we'll put our efforts into preparing for battle.

MALCOLM
Cousins, I hope the days are near at hand
That chambers will be safe.

MENTEITH
We doubt it nothing.

SIWARD
What wood is this before us?

MENTEITH
The Wood of Birnam.

MALCOLM
Let every soldier hew him down a bough,
And bear't before him: thereby shall we shadow
The numbers of our host, and make discovery
Err in report of us.

SOLDIERS
It shall be done.

SIWARD
We learn no other but the confident tyrant
Keeps still in Dunsinane, and will endure
Our setting down before't.

MALCOLM
'Tis his main hope;
For where there is advantage to be given,
Both more and less have given him the revolt,
And none serve with him but constrained things
Whose hearts are absent too.

MACDUFF
Let our just censures
Attend the true event, and put we on
Industrious soldiership.

SIWARD

The time approaches.

Soon enough the odds will show,

What we're due and what we owe

We can speculate until we are hoarse

But such issues are settled only by force.

Saying which, forward to battle!

SIWARD

The time approaches

That will with due decision make us know

What we shall say we have and what we owe.

Thoughts speculative their unsure hopes relate,

But certain issue strokes must arbitrate;

Towards which, advance the war.

THEY ALL CHEER AND MARCH OFF.

ACT V SCENE V

THE COURT OF CASTLE DUNSINANE.

BACK IN THE CASTLE, MACBETH, SETON, AND THE DOCTOR CONTINUE
THEIR CONVERSATION, MACBETH NOW WEARING ARMOUR.

MACBETH	MACBETH
Hang our banners on the outer walls. The news is still, "They're coming!" The strength of our castle makes a mockery of their siege. Let them lay in wait until they are consumed by famine and plague. Had they not been reinforced by our own men we might have dared meet them face to face and beat them back home to England.	Hang out our banners on the outward walls; The cry is still, "They come": Our castle's strength Will laugh a siege to scorn. Here let them lie Till famine and the ague eat them up. Were they not forced with those that should be ours, We might have met them dareful, beard to beard, And beat them backward home.

A WOMAN'S LOUD SCREAM IS HEARD, THEN WAILING WOMEN.

MACBETH (CONT'D)	MACBETH
What is that noise?	What is that noise?
SETON	**SEYTON**
Women crying, my lord.	It is the cry of women, my good lord.

THE DOCTOR EXITS HURRIEDLY TO INVESTIGATE, SETON FOLLOWS.

MACBETH	MACBETH
(*to self*) I'd almost forgotten the taste of fear. There was a time my senses would be chilled to hear a scream in the night, my hair standing on end as if alive at such a mournful sound. I've had my fill of horrors; atrocities are now so commonplace in my murderous thoughts they no longer move me.	I have almost forgot the taste of fears: The time has been, my senses would have cool'd To hear a night-shriek, and my fell of hair Would at a dismal treatise rouse and stir As life were in't: I have supp'd full with horrors; Direness, familiar to my slaughterous thoughts, Cannot once start me.

SETON RETURNS.

MACBETH (CONT'D)	MACBETH
(*to Seton*) Why all the crying?	Wherefore was that cry?
SETON	**SEYTON**
It's the Queen, my lord. She's dead.	The Queen, my lord, is dead.

Act V Scene V. Castle Dunsinane.

MACBETH

She had to die sometime. There had to
come a day to use such a word.
Tomorrow, and tomorrow, and
tomorrow, day by day creeping slowly
towards the last breath of time. With all
our yesterdays merely lighting the way
for fools to reach their dusty graves.
Out, out, short candle! Life's nothing
but a walking illusion, a wretched actor
who struts and frets his hour upon the
stage and then is heard no more. A tale
told by an idiot, loud and furious, but
with no meaning.

MACBETH

She should have died hereafter;
There would have been a time for such a word.
Tomorrow, and tomorrow, and tomorrow
Creeps in this petty pace from day to day
To the last syllable of recorded time;
And all our yesterdays have lighted fools
The way to dusty death. Out, out, brief candle!
Life's but a walking shadow, a poor player
That struts and frets his hour upon the stage
And then is heard no more. It is a tale
Told by an idiot, full of sound and fury,
Signifying nothing.

Note: This is a famous speech, and Macbeth's seventh and final soliloquy,
extracts from which are often quoted. However it is also a problem speech.
There are four possible meanings to the first line, (listed below) the meaning of
which, determines the mood and meaning of the lines which follow. It
determines whether he cares about her death or shrugs it off as having to
happen sometime; tomorrow, or the day after, each day bringing us another
day closer to the inevitable, making our existence almost worthless. Or is he
saying she should have shared in his victory and died later when they could
have mourned her loss properly?

Whichever way you read it, it suggests he now feels the inevitable is coming
and without her he is destined to lose everything. It is also possible to combine
all four meanings and still make sense of what is said. (The second line doesn't
help, being equally ambiguous).

1, she should have died after the battle, after my victory, then we could mourn
properly. 2, she should have waited and died with me. 3, she had to die
sometime, either now or later. 4, she should have died after the battle, for now,
with her gone, I know I will not win.

A MESSENGER ARRIVES, HE SEES MACBETH'S WILD LOOK AND HESITATES.

MACBETH (CONT'D)

(snarled) You came to use your tongue;
use it, quickly.

MESSENGER

(scared) My gracious Lord, I should
report what I saw, but I'm not sure how
to.

MACBETH

Just say it, man!

MACBETH

Thou comest to use thy tongue; thy story
quickly.

MESSENGER

Gracious my lord,
I should report that which I say I saw,
But know not how to do it.

MACBETH

Well, say, sir.

MESSENGER From my observation point on the hill, I looked towards Birnam, and right there, I thought I saw the wood begin to move.	**MESSENGER** As I did stand my watch upon the hill, I look'd toward Birnam, and anon, methought, The Wood began to move.
MACBETH (*raising his arm to strike*) You are a liar and a fool!	**MACBETH** Liar and slave!
MESSENGER (*cowering*) May your wrath be unleashed upon me if it's not true. Less than three miles away, you can see it coming. I tell you, a moving grove.	**MESSENGER** Let me suffer your anger if it isn't so. Within these three miles, you can see it coming, I say, a moving grove.
MACBETH If you're lying, you'll be hung alive from the nearest tree till you starve to death. If you speak the truth, I won't care if you do the same to me.	**MACBETH** If thou speak'st false, Upon the next tree shalt thou hang alive, Till famine cling thee; if thy speech be sooth, I care not if thou dost for me as much.

THE MESSENGER FLEES.

MACBETH (CONT'D) (*to self*) I'm losing my resolve, and beginning to doubt the *'equivocation'* of the fiend whose lies sounded so convincing. "*Fear not,*" he said, "*Till Birnam Wood comes to Dunsinane.*" And now a wood moves towards Dunsinane. (*calling*) To arms, to arms! Everybody out!	**MACBETH** I pull in resolution and begin To doubt the equivocation of the fiend That lies like truth. "Fear not, till Birnam Wood Do come to Dunsinane," and now a wood Comes toward Dunsinane. Arm, arm, and out!

Note: Yet another reference to the priest who 'equivocated' – lied under oath – during the trial for the Gunpowder Plot to assassinate the King.

MACBETH (CONT'D) (*to self*) If that which he professes does appear, There is no fleeing, nor loitering here. I begin to grow weary of the sun, The world can end now with us all undone. -- (*calling*) Ring the alarm bell! (*to self*) Let ill winds blow, bringing ruin and wrack! At least we'll die with armour on our back.	**MACBETH** If this which he avouches does appear, There is nor flying hence nor tarrying here. I 'gin to be aweary of the sun And wish the estate o' the world were now undone. Ring the alarum bell! Blow, wind! Come, wrack! At least we'll die with harness on our back.

HE STORMS OUT OF THE ROOM IN HIS ARMOUR.

Note: Macbeth realises he is in a 'no win' situation now that the Witches' prophecy has been undone. He had planned to withstand a siege. Going out to meet his opponents throws away his last chance, it gives his remaining men the opportunity to desert him and brings him face to face with the man who is destined to slay him.

ACT V SCENE VI

THE CASTLE GATE AT DUNSINANE.

MALCOLM, SIWARD, AND MACDUFF LEAD THE ARMY CARRYING TREE
BRANCHES TO THE CASTLE GATE. IT IS OPEN FROM EVERYONE FLEEING.

PRINCE MALCOLM	MALCOLM
We are close enough now. Throw down your leafy disguise and show yourselves as you are! My honourable uncle, Lord Siward, shall lead the first onslaught with his noble son, while the honourable Macduff and I shall take care of the rest, as we planned.	Now near enough; your leavy screens throw down, And show like those you are. You, worthy uncle, Shall, with my cousin, your right noble son, Lead our first battle. Worthy Macduff and we Shall take upon's what else remains to do, According to our order.
SIWARD	**SIWARD**
Good luck, men. *If we can find the tyrant's forces tonight, Let us be beaten if we don't stand and fight.*	Fare you well. *Do we but find the tyrant's power tonight, Let us be beaten, if we cannot fight.*
MACDUFF	**MACDUFF**
Sound all our trumpets! Give them all breath, Those raucous announcers of blood and of death!	*Make all our trumpets speak; give them all breath, Those clamorous harbingers of blood and death.*

MALCOLM RAISES HIS ARM.

HE DROPS IT SHARPLY AND THE TRUMPETS SOUND THE ATTACK.

THE MEN STORM THE CASTLE.

Note: Siward says 'tonight', suggesting they are attacking late in the day, or perhaps he means it will be over by the end of the day.

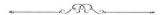

ACT V SCENE VII

LARGE HALL IN THE CASTLE.

MACBETH ENTERS THE HALL ALONE. FROM ELSEWHERE COMES THE LOUD
NOISE OF MEN IN BATTLE AND TRUMPETING.

MACBETH	MACBETH
They've tied me to a stake; there's no escape. Like a chained bear I must stay and fight. But what man is not born of woman? That's the only one I need fear, no other.	They have tied me to a stake; I cannot fly, But bear-like I must fight the course. What's he That was not born of woman? Such a one Am I to fear, or none.

Note: Bear baiting was once a common sport. It is known that there was a bear used for such purposes outside the Globe theatre. Shakespeare wrote the bear into plays as it was conveniently placed. The sport comprised a bear chained to a stake upon which dogs were set loose to 'bait' it – attack it, forcing it to defend itself. 'Course' was a single session of the sport, like a 'round' in boxing, where the bear had no option but to fight or be killed.

ENTER YOUNG SIWARD BRANDISHING HIS SWORD.

MACBETH STOPS AND LOOKS AT HIM WITH CONTEMPT.

Note: This was Young Siward's first battle, one of the 'whiskerless' (without a beard) youths, putting him between the ages of 14-17.

YOUNG SIWARD	YOUNG SIWARD
What is your name?	What is thy name?
MACBETH	MACBETH
A name you'd be afraid to hear.	Thou'lt be afraid to hear it.
YOUNG SIWARD	YOUNG SIWARD
Never! Even if you had a name from the depths of hell itself.	No, though thou call'st thyself a hotter name Than any is in hell.
MACBETH	MACBETH
My name is Macbeth.	My name's Macbeth.
YOUNG SIWARD	YOUNG SIWARD:
The devil himself could not utter a name more hateful to my ear.	The devil himself could not pronounce a title More hateful to mine ear.
MACBETH	MACBETH
No. Nor more frightening.	No, nor more fearful.

YOUNG SIWARD

You lie, you loathsome tyrant! And I'll prove the lie with my sword.

YOUNG SIWARD

Thou liest, abhorred tyrant; with my sword
I'll prove the lie thou speak'st.

THEY FIGHT AND YOUNG SIWARD IS KILLED WITH A LOUD EXCLAMATION.

MACBETH SPEAKS TO THE LIFELESS YOUNG BODY.

MACBETH

You were born of woman.
Swords and weapons I laugh at in scorn,
When brandished by men of woman born.

MACBETH

Thou wast born of woman.
But swords I smile at, weapons laugh to scorn,
Brandish'd by man that's of a woman born.

MACBETH CALMLY LEAVES BY A SIDE DOOR AS THE SOUND OF FIGHTING
DRAWS CLOSER AND CLOSER.

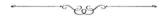

A COURTYARD OF THE CASTLE.

MACDUFF HEARS LOUD FIGHTING FROM WITHIN THE CASTLE, HE IS
DESPERATE TO BE THE ONE WHO KILLS MACBETH.

MACDUFF

The noise is coming from that way. (*shouting*) Tyrant! Show your face! If you are not killed by my hand, the ghosts of my wife and children will forever haunt me! I'll not fight wretched foot soldiers paid to wield their pikes. It's either you, Macbeth, or my sword returns to its sheath unblemished.
(*he listens*) You must be over there, the mighty clatter indicates someone of high rank. Fortune, let it be me who finds him! I beg for nothing more.

MACDUFF

That way the noise is. Tyrant, show thy face!
If thou beest slain and with no stroke of mine,
My wife and children's ghosts will haunt me still.
I cannot strike at wretched kerns, whose arms
Are hired to bear their staves. Either thou, Macbeth,
Or else my sword, with an unbatter'd edge,
I sheathe again undeeded. There thou shouldst be;
By this great clatter, one of greatest note
Seems bruited. Let me find him, fortune!
And more I beg not.

MACDUFF LEAVES ALONE.

FROM THE DIRECTION OF THE SHOUTING, OLD SIWARD ENTERS WITH
SOME MEN AND CALLS TO PRINCE MALCOLM.

SIWARD

This way, my lord. The castle's defences were easily overcome. The tyrant's men fight on both sides. *Our noble lords prove brave in war; The day itself is almost yours.* There's little left to do.

PRINCE MALCOLM

Foes we meet turn and fight beside us.

SIWARD

Enter the castle, sir.

SIWARD

This way, my lord; the castle's gently render'd. The tyrant's people on both sides do fight, *The noble thanes do bravely in the war; The day almost itself professes yours,* And little is to do.

MALCOLM

We have met with foes That strike beside us.

SIWARD

Enter, sir, the castle.

THEY ENTER THE CASTLE.

ACT V SCENE VIII

Castle Banqueting Hall.

MACBETH SITS ALONE AT THE HEAD OF THE BANQUETING TABLE.
THE SAME TABLE BANQUO'S GHOST APPEARED AT.

THE SOUND OF FIGHTING ECHOES FROM OUTSIDE THE HALL.

Note: In the original text there was no scene division here.

MACBETH
(aside) Why should I play the Roman fool and die by my own sword? While I still see men alive, the gashes are better suited to them.

MACBETH
Why should I play the Roman fool and die
On mine own sword? Whiles I see lives, the gashes
Do better upon them.

Note: By 'Roman fool' he means the practice of Roman leaders who killed themselves after losing a battle.

MACDUFF ENTERS THE ROOM FROM BEHIND WHERE MACBETH SITS.

MACBETH IS SURPRISINGLY UNMOVED BY THE EVENTS HAPPENING AROUND HIM. HE DOESN'T NOTICE MACDUFF ENTER.

MACDUFF
Turn, hell-hound. Turn!

MACDUFF
Turn, hell hound, turn!

MACBETH SLOWLY TURNS IN HIS SEAT, HIS SWORD LIES ON THE TABLE, THE HANDLE STILL IN HIS HAND.

MACBETH
Of all men, it is you I have avoided. Come no closer, my soul is too full of the blood of your kin already.

MACBETH
Of all men else I have avoided thee.
But get thee back; my soul is too much charged
With blood of thine already.

MACDUFF
I have no words for you, villain! My sword will speak for me, mere words could not begin to describe your evil!

MACDUFF
I have no words:
My voice is in my sword, thou bloodier villain
Than terms can give thee out!

THEY FIGHT. MACBETH WITH CONFIDENT EASE, MACDUFF WITH DESPERATION AND REVENGE DRIVING HIM.

MACBETH

You waste your energy. You'll find it easier to wound the air with your keen sword than make me bleed. Let your blade fall on vulnerable heads, I bear a charmed life which cannot be taken by one born of woman.

MACBETH

Thou losest labor.
As easy mayst thou the intrenchant air
With thy keen sword impress as make me bleed:
Let fall thy blade on vulnerable crests;
I bear a charmed life, which must not yield
To one of woman born.

MACDUFF CATCHES MACBETH A GLANCING BLOW WHICH
CAUSES HIM TO BLEED IN DEFIANCE OF HIS OWN WORDS.

MACBETH LOOKS SURPRISED.

MACDUFF

Your charm is useless. Tell the fallen angel who protects you this;
(*slow and meaningfully*) Macduff was from his mother's womb prematurely ripped.

MACDUFF

Despair thy charm,
And let the angel whom thou still hast served
Tell thee, Macduff was from his mother's womb
Untimely ripp'd.

MACBETH'S COURAGE DROPS LIKE A STONE. HE STEPS BACK.

NOW, FOR THE FIRST TIME, MACBETH HAS TO FIGHT FOR HIS LIFE
WITHOUT HIS DEFIANT CONFIDENCE.

MACBETH

Cursed be the tongue that tells me this! It makes me less of a man. These word juggling demons toy with us in their double meanings. They give promise of hope in our ear, then turn around and destroy it.

MACBETH

Accursed be that tongue that tells me so,
For it hath cow'd my better part of man!
And be these juggling fiends no more believed,
That palter with us in a double sense,
That keep the word of promise to our ear,
And break it to our hope.

MACBETH LOWERS HIS SWORD.

MACBETH (CONT'D)
I'll not fight you.

MACBETH
I'll not fight with thee.

MACDUFF

Then surrender, coward, and live to be put on show and gawped at the rest of your days. We'll put you in a freak show, your picture on a pole with the caption - "Come see the tyrant here."

MACDUFF

Then yield thee, coward,
And live to be the show and gaze o' the time.
We'll have thee, as our rarer monsters are,
Painted upon a pole, and underwrit,
"Here may you see the tyrant."

MACBETH	MACBETH
I will not surrender, to kiss the ground beneath young Malcolm's feet, and be taunted by the curses of the rabble. Though Birnam Wood has come to Dunsinane, and you, my opponent, are not born of woman, I will fight to the end! *I raise my shield, so fight on, Macduff,* *And damned be the one who first cries,* *'Enough!'*	I will not yield, To kiss the ground before young Malcolm's feet, And to be baited with the rabble's curse. Though Birnam Wood be come to Dunsinane, And thou opposed, being of no woman born, Yet I will try the last. Before my body *I throw my warlike shield! Lay on, Macduff,* *And damn'd be him that first cries, "Hold, enough!"*

THEY FIGHT BUT WE DO NOT SEE THE END OF THE FIGHT IN THIS SCENE.

> Note: The famous quote of "Lead on, Macduff" is a misquote from this passage of Macbeth. The correct words were, "Lay on, Macduff", which has the altogether different meaning of starting to fight. This misquote has been around for at least two centuries.

ACT V SCENE IX

THE CASTLE COURTYARD.

MALCOLM, SIWARD, AND ROSS GATHER IN THE COURTYARD.
SOLDIERS SWARM AROUND. SOUNDS OF SUBDUED FIGHTING.

BUGLES SOUND THE RETREAT (SIGNIFYING THE BATTLE IS OVER).

TRUMPETS SOUND THE ROYAL ANNOUNCEMENT FROM MALCOLM.

Note: Again, there was no scene break here in the original text.

PRINCE MALCOLM
My hopes are that our missing friends got through this safely.

SIWARD
Some must have died, and yet, by those I can see, such a great victory was cheaply bought.

PRINCE MALCOLM
Macduff is missing. And Young Siward, your noble son.

LORD ROSS
Your son, my lord, has paid a soldier's debt. Though he barely lived to be a man, he died like a man, proving his fighting prowess with a fearless stand.

SIWARD
Then he is confirmed dead?

LORD ROSS
Aye, he was carried from the battlefield. Do not measure your sorrow by his worthiness, for then your sorrow would have no end.

SIWARD
Were his wounds to his front?

LORD ROSS
Aye, to the front

MALCOLM
I would the friends we miss were safe arrived.

SIWARD
Some must go off: and yet, by these I see,
So great a day as this is cheaply bought.

MALCOLM
Macduff is missing, and your noble son.

ROSS
Your son, my lord, has paid a soldier's debt:
He only lived but till he was a man;
The which no sooner had his prowess confirm'd
In the unshrinking station where he fought,
But like a man he died.

SIWARD
Then he is dead?

ROSS
Ay, and brought off the field. Your cause of sorrow
Must not be measured by his worth, for then
It hath no end.

SIWARD
Had he his hurts before?

ROSS
Ay, on the front.

SIWARD	SIWARD
Truly one of God's soldiers! Had I as many sons as I have hairs, I could not wish them a nobler death. And so his death bell is tolled.	Why then, God's soldier be he! Had I as many sons as I have hairs, I would not wish them to a fairer death. And so his knell is knoll'd.

PRINCE MALCOLM	MALCOLM
He deserves more acclaim, and that I shall give him.	He's worth more sorrow, And that I'll spend for him.

SIWARD	SIWARD
He has all he needs, they say he died bravely and did his duty. God be with him!	He's worth no more: They say he parted well and paid his score: And so God be with him!

Note: 'Paid off his score' (or settled a debt) also means to avenge a wrong as well as did his duty (and paid the price with his life).

MACDUFF ENTERS CARRYING MACBETH'S HEAD.

SIWARD (CONT'D)	SIWARD
Look. Here comes fresh comfort.	Here comes newer comfort.

MACDUFF	MACDUFF:
(approaching) Hail, King Malcolm! - for that you now are. Behold the usurper, Macbeth's accursed head!	Hail, King! for so thou art. Behold where stands The usurper's cursed head.

MACDUFF RAISES THE HEAD ALOFT FOR ALL TO SEE.

MACDUFF (CONT'D)	MACDUFF:
We are freed. I see you surrounded by your loyal Lords, the pearls of your Kingdom. One and all they share in my sentiment. I call upon them now to join voice with me in, 'Hail, King of Scotland!'	The time is free. I see thee compass'd with thy kingdom's pearl That speak my salutation in their minds, Whose voices I desire aloud with mine: Hail, King of Scotland!

ALL	ALL
Hail, King of Scotland!	Hail, King of Scotland!

TRUMPETS SOUND IN TRIUMPH.

MACDUFF THROWS THE HEAD LIKE A FOOTBALL TO A SOLDIER WITH A
PIKE, THE SOLDIER IMPALES THE HEAD ON THE PIKE AND WAVES IT ALOFT
FOR ALL TO SEE AND CHEER.

PRINCE MALCOLM

I shall not keep you waiting long before reckoning my debts with you all and settling them in full. My lords and fellow kinsmen, henceforth to be earls, the first Scotland ever named in such an honour. There is much to do with this new beginning, such as calling home our exiled friends who fled the snares of this evil tyranny, and hunting down the cruel agents of this dead butcher and his evil queen, who, they say, took her own life with those murderous hands of hers.

This we will see, by God's own grace,
Performed at the proper time and place.
So in thanks to all and in turn to each one,
I invite you to see me be crowned at Scone.

MALCOLM

We shall not spend a large expense of time
Before we reckon with your several loves,
And make us even with you. My thanes and
  kinsmen,
Henceforth be Earls, the first that ever Scotland
In such an honor named. What's more to do,
Which would be planted newly with the time,
As calling home our exiled friends abroad
That fled the snares of watchful tyranny,
Producing forth the cruel ministers
Of this dead butcher and his fiend-like queen,
Who, as 'tis thought, by self and violent hands
Took off her life; this, and what needful else

That calls upon us, by the grace of Grace
We will perform in measure, time, and place,
So thanks to all at once and to each one,
Whom we invite to see us crown'd at Scone.

THE LORDS CHEER.

THE END

32559811R00102